Medical Symptoms not Explained by Organic Disease

Edited by
FRANCIS CREED
RICHARD MAYOU
ANTHONY HOPKINS

Medical Symptoms not Explained by Organic Disease

THE ROYAL COLLEGE OF PSYCHIATRISTS &
THE ROYAL COLLEGE OF PHYSICIANS OF LONDON

Distributed in North America
by American Psychiatric Press, Inc.
ISBN 0 88048 609 0

British Library Cataloguing-in-Publication Data

Medical symptoms not explained by organic disease.
I. Creed, Francis   II. Mayou, Richard
III. Hopkins, Anthony, *1937*–
610

ISBN 0-902241-42-7

Phototypeset by Dobbie Typesetting Limited, Tavistock, Devon
Printed in Great Britain by
Henry Ling Limited, Dorchester, Dorset

Contents

Contributors

Christopher Bass, Consultant Liaison Psychiatrist, Department of Psychological Medicine, John Radcliffe Hospital, Headington, Oxford OX3 9DU

John Chambers, Lecturer, Department of Cardiology, Guy's Hospital, St Thomas's St, London SE1 9RT

Francis Creed, Senior Lecturer and Honorary Consultant Psychiatrist, University Department of Psychiatry, Rawnsley Buildings, Manchester Royal Infirmary, Oxford Road, Manchester M13 9WL

Charlotte Feinmann, Senior Lecturer and Consultant Psychiatrist, University College and Middlesex School of Medicine and the Institute of Dental Surgery, Eastman Dental Hospital, 256 Gray's Inn Road, London WC1 8LD

David Goldberg, Professor of Psychiatry, Director, Mental Illness Research Unit, Withington Hospital, West Didsbury, Manchester M20 8LR

Elspeth Guthrie, Senior Registrar in Psychotherapy, Manchester Royal Infirmary, Gaskell House, Swinton Grove, Manchester M13

Kenneth Heaton, Reader in Medicine and Consultant Physician, Bristol Royal Infirmary, Bristol BS2 8HW

Anthony Hopkins, Director, Research Unit, Royal College of Physicians, 11 St Andrew's Place, London NW1 4LE

Richard Mayou, Clinical Reader in Psychiatry, University Department of Psychiatry, Warneford Hospital, Oxford OX3 7JX

Paul Salkovskis, Research Clinical Psychologist, University of Oxford, Department of Psychiatry, Warneford Hospital, Headington, Oxford OX3 7JX

Preface

ANDREW SIMS and
MARGARET TURNER-WARWICK

Many patients have symptoms that worry them, yet which on full analysis do not prove to be firmly linked to organic medical disease. Examples include chest pain of non-cardiac origin, abdominal pain, breathlessness, fatigue and headache. Physicians are perhaps too ready to see their role as ruling out structural disease requiring some technical medical or surgical intervention, rather than providing the explanation and reassurance which allows these patients to tolerate their symptoms more readily. In order to encourage a better framework for the management of these patients, our two Colleges held a Conference at the Royal College of Physicians. This book is the child of that Conference, which we warmly commend to all physicians and psychiatrists. Dr Francis Creed, Dr Richard Mayou and Dr Anthony Hopkins have done our patients and colleagues a service in exploring the problems of patients who have symptoms for which no clear-cut organic cause can be demonstrated. The editors and chapter authors review the substantial body of research which shows how these patients can be effectively and humanely cared for, often without the need for extensive investigation or, indeed, for extensive psychological assessment.

Our two Colleges are exploring ways in which we can improve the training of physicians in psychiatry and psychiatrists in medicine, and in improving the status of liaison psychiatry in general hospitals.

Andrew Sims
President, Royal College of Psychiatrists

Margaret Turner-Warwick
President, Royal College of Physicians of London

Introduction

FRANCIS CREED, RICHARD MAYOU and ANTHONY HOPKINS

Non-organic physical symptoms such as abdominal pain, headache and atypical chest pain are common in all medical settings. They are also frequent in the general population. Usually such symptoms are transient and of little significance, and many people with such symptoms do not consult doctors. Those who do so are generally reassured that the symptoms do not represent underlying organic disease. Some patients, however, are not reassured; they continue to experience symptoms and may become increasingly concerned about them. Management of these complaints makes up a substantial proportion of consultations in general practice, and those with persistent symptoms may be referred to out-patient clinics. Non-specific symptom diagnoses are among the most common out-patient diagnoses. Investigations and further reassurance are frequently ineffective, and continuing symptoms may cause distress and disability.

This book is concerned with the nature of these complaints, their aetiology, and their management. We have tried to avoid confusing and often pejorative jargon which obscures understanding. Labels such as 'hypochondriacal', 'hysterical', and 'functional overlay' are often used without specific meaning. In this book, we refer to these complaints as non-organic symptoms, because they are frequently defined by exclusion. Investigations demonstrate the absence of organic disease, but a positive diagnosis has yet to be made. We also do our best to avoid explanations which use numerous overlapping technical terms for the psychological processes involved. The terms 'attribution' and 'interpretation' are used interchangeably to describe the process of patients' understanding of their physical perceptions.

Chapters 1–6 describe different aspects of the aetiology and presentation of these complaints. Our contributors – physicians and psychiatrists – write from varied clinical standpoints but share a belief that non-organic symptoms are common, that they pose a major clinical problem, and that they are generally poorly managed by doctors at present. They argue that physical, psychological and social factors interact in both causation and presentation of symptoms, so that a complete understanding of all aetiological factors is important for appropriate assessment and management. Central to the management of non-organic symptoms is a convincing explanation to the patient about the origin and nature of the symptoms. Psychiatric disorders such as anxiety and depression are common, but wider psychological factors, relating to an individual's knowledge and beliefs, are also important in our understanding of these disorders. All contributors stress the importance of accepting the reality of the symptoms at the outset, of considering psychological factors at the initial assessment, and of carefully preparing the way towards referral to special services if necessary.

In the first chapter, Dr Heaton distinguishes abdominal symptoms which are common in the general population, and which are not taken to the doctor, from similar symptoms in patients who attend a gastroenterology clinic. In Chapter 2, Dr Creed indicates the role of distressing life events and psychiatric disorder in precipitating these symptoms. In the case of headache, Dr Hopkins contrasts the traditional role of medical investigations, which are nearly always negative, with the more positive approach of attempting to understand the patient's concerns and to provide an explanation for the symptom.

Dr Chambers, a physician, and Dr Bass, a psychiatrist, writing about atypical chest pain, criticise the common exhaustive search for cardiac disease, and indicate the poor outcome following negative coronary angiography. They suggest a variety of possible physical causes which should be considered. They also demonstrate the positive role of psychological factors in the causation of atypical chest pain and indicate how understanding these factors can improve management. Dr Mayou develops the concept of an interaction between physical and psychological factors in causing symptoms and demonstrates how both may be important for satisfactory treatment.

Because of the diverse nature of these non-organic symptoms and their explanation, the first part of this book concludes with a summary of the themes common to all, and suggests a model which can be applied to clinical assessment.

The second half of the book is principally concerned with treatments which have been demonstrated to be effective in relieving non-organic physical symptoms. It is important to present this evidence as many doctors remain sceptical about the efficacy of psychological treatments for these complaints. In order to proceed to any form of psychological treatment, however, the doctor must first help patients to appreciate the psychological basis of their somatic symptoms. Professor Goldberg has developed such a model for general practice, which he describes in Chapter 7. His video-taped teaching programme has been shown to be effective in teaching general practitioners the appropriate skills. A similar model needs to be developed for the training of physicians.

The remaining chapters describe different aspects of treatment used by psychiatrists and psychologists. It is from these specialist treatments that a simplified model might be derived which physicians can use in the medical out-patient clinic. Dr Guthrie indicates how the interpersonal difficulties of the patient with refractory irritable bowel syndrome can also cause problems in the relationship with the doctor. If these problems are tackled directly in a trusting psychotherapeutic relationship, patients may be able to discuss and understand their worries, a process which is often accompanied by symptomatic improvement.

Dr Salkovskis describes the ingredients of cognitive behavioural treatment, which emphasises the importance of understanding patients' underlying attitudes and beliefs about their symptoms, if these are to be modified. This approach has been widely used in the treatment of anxiety disorders in psychiatric settings. Dr Salkovskis shows that his methods can be applied to patients who are anxious about physical complaints. While he is particularly concerned with a small minority of patients with chronic and disabling hypochondriacal problems, the principles can be more widely applied.

Dr Feinmann uses the model of atypical facial pain to illustrate the role of antidepressive drugs. These can be useful, not only for their primary action on depressed mood but also probably for analgesic and anxiolytic actions. Antidepressants have been widely used by neurologists, rheumatologists and doctors working in pain clinics. It is clear that they have an important role in the management of some types of non-organic symptoms.

The following chapters describe various approaches to treatment but cannot be comprehensive. They illustrate the current state of specialist treatments, which have been systematically evaluated. Such methods of treatment need to be developed and refined to provide all physicians with a general model of assessment and treatment that can be used in the out-patient clinic. We hope that this book will help stimulate physicians and psychiatrists to join together in this task.

1 What makes people with abdominal pain consult their doctor?

KENNETH HEATON

The answer to the question posed in the title of this chapter is considered in three parts:

(a) How many people in the community get recurrent or chronic abdominal pain?
(b) How many people with such pain consult a doctor?
(c) What are the differences between those who consult doctors and those who do not?

How many people get recurrent or chronic abdominal pain?

Epidemiological data about this are limited. In Arctic Norway, as part of the Tromsø Heart Study, 14 102 people were asked the question "Do you often suffer from cramping abdominal pain?" A positive answer was given by 11% of men and 17% of women (Johnsen et al, 1986). In three-quarters of these people the pain was probably due to irritable bowel syndrome (IBS) because the subjects also admitted frequent abdominal bloating and rumbling.

One weakness of the Tromsø study is that there was no standard definition of 'often'. Several smaller surveys agreed to define recurrent abdominal pain as pain occurring on more than six days in the past year. These were not proper epidemiological surveys but studies of selected groups of healthy people such as students, and the results are reasonably consistent (Table 1.1), namely that at least 20% of healthy people admit to recurrent abdominal pain and in most of them the pain has the features of IBS.

To show that this is true of the general public, we need data from a random sample of the population. A study has been carried out in Bristol using a stratified random sample of 1058 women and 838 men (O'Donnell et al, 1990).

TABLE 1.1

Prevalence (%) of recurrent abdominal pain (>6 days in the past year) in surveys of apparently healthy people in different countries

Country	Number questioned	Abdominal pain	Colonic pain	Reference
England	301	20	14	Thompson & Heaton (1980)
France	1200	no data	14	Bommelaer *et al* (1986)
USA	789	24	22	Drossman *et al* (1982)
New Zealand	287	no data	14	Welch *et al* (1985)
China	233	29	23	Bi-zhen & Qi-Ying (1988)

Recurrent abdominal pain (other than menstrual) was admitted to by 25% of women and there was no variation with age in the range studied, namely, 25–69 years. The rate was somewhat less in men (16%). In 80% of women with abdominal pain and in 62% of men with abdominal pain there were features to suggest IBS.

How many people with recurrent abdominal pain consult a doctor?

Several published studies of the prevalence of IBS have included a question about consulting a doctor. The percentage of IBS sufferers who had seen a doctor in these studies varied between 23% and 47% (Thompson & Heaton, 1980; Drossman *et al*, 1982, 1986; Sandler *et al*, 1984). Thus most people with IBS, and by inference most people with recurrent abdominal pain, do not consult a doctor about it.

The published consultation rates are probably an overestimate because, according to a recent prospective study (Heaton *et al*, 1991), most episodes of abdominal pain are ignored or forgotten, at least in women. The 27 women in Heaton *et al*'s study, all aged 20–39 years, had taken part in the Bristol survey and so had been asked if they ever had abdominal pain. All had denied it. For a month they kept symptom diaries and were telephoned every few days to encourage compliance and to provide more information about abdominal pain and bloating. Surprisingly, 81% of these pain-deniers experienced one or more episodes of pain during the month.

Extrapolating from these data and from the Bristol survey, it can be calculated that, of every 100 women aged 20–39, 80 get recurrent abdominal pain but about 56 forget about it. Of the 24 who remember their pain, about 14 do not bother to tell their doctors about it, leaving just 10 who do see a doctor (Fig. 1.1). Thus only one in eight women with recurrent abdominal pain consult their doctor about it.

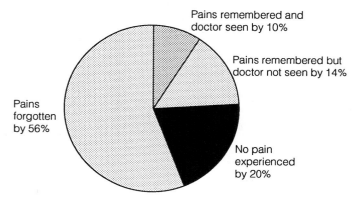

Pains remembered and doctor seen by 10%

Pains remembered but doctor not seen by 14%

Pains forgotten by 56%

No pain experienced by 20%

Fig. 1.1. Prevalence of recurrent abdominal pain in women aged 20–39 years

What are the differences between consulters and non-consulters?

These data tempt one to suggest that people who have pains and do consult doctors are those who complain or worry most. However, other data show it is not that simple. The prospective study included 26 women, matched for age, who had been referred to a gastroenterology clinic and diagnosed as having IBS. In these women, abdominal pains were much more frequent than in the pain-deniers, referred to above. During the month the median number of pain episodes per person was 13 in the patients and only three in the pain-deniers. Furthermore, severity ratings given to these pains tended to be higher in the patients. To quantify the pain burden we calculated a weighted pain score as follows:

Weighted pain score = $P_1 + 2P_2 + 3P_3 + 4P_4$
where P_1 = no. of episodes in 31 days of *mild* pain (grade 1, can be ignored)
P_2 = no. of episodes of *moderate* pain (grade 2, distracting somewhat from work or leisure)
P_3 = no. of episodes of *severe* pain (grade 3, making the subject stop what she was doing)
P_4 = no. of episodes of *incapacitating* pain (grade 4, forcing her to lie down)

The weighted pain score was far higher in the patients than in the pain-deniers, namely 32.5 versus 4.0 (median values). The pain-deniers presumably had so little pain that they forgot it or considered it of no importance.

Patients with IBS have other symptoms besides pain, especially bloating or distension and symptoms of abnormal defaecation like urgency and

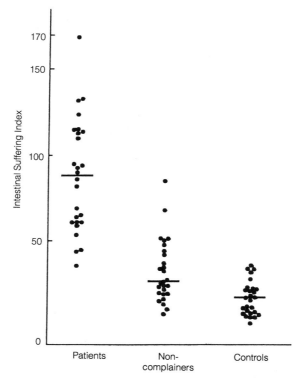

Fig. 1.2. 'Intestinal suffering index' in three groups of young women – patients with IBS, people who have IBS but have not seen a doctor about it (non-complainers) and people who had previously denied having abdominal pain (controls). The index is an expression of IBS symptoms experienced over a 31-day prospective study period, the chief contributor to the index being abdominal pain (Heaton et al, 1991)

feelings of incomplete evacuation. To obtain an estimate of their total symptom load we calculated an 'intestinal suffering index' as the sum of three factors: weighted pain score, number of episodes of bloating in 31 days, and number of abnormal defaecations in 31 days. An abnormal defaecation was defined as one associated with urgency or incomplete evacuation.

Figure 1.2 shows that the intestinal suffering index was markedly higher in the patients with IBS than in the pain-deniers ($P<0.001$).

The point that patients with IBS really have something to complain about is underscored by other data included in Fig. 1.2, namely the findings in 27 young women whom we call non-complainers, non-consulters or non-patients. These are women who took part in our epidemiological survey and who admitted to recurrent abdominal pain of intestinal origin, that is to say pain which lessened with defaecation, but who denied having seen a doctor about it. In these women, the intestinal suffering index or symptom load was significantly less than that of the consulters ($P<0.001$) although there was some overlap.

Non-complainers can be considered as pain-rememberers (or pain-admitters) as opposed to the control group who are pain-deniers and, in most cases, pain-forgetters. The weighted pain score of pain-admitters was more than that of the pain-deniers (median 10 v. 4 in the pain-deniers ($P<0.001$)), which presumably helps to explain why they remembered and so admitted having pain. At the same time, the fact that they had so much less pain than the patients with IBS presumably helps to explain why they had not become patients.

If it is the sheer burden of symptoms which drives people to their doctors then there should be, in the population, a relationship between the number of symptoms of IBS and the consulting rate. We looked at this in our survey and found that there is indeed such a relationship (Fig. 1.3). The slope of the regression line relating these two variables is the same in women and men, which implies that women are no more prone to consult doctors about IBS than are men. The fact that more women consult doctors is simply because more women get IBS.

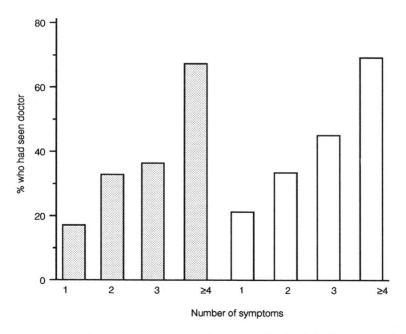

Fig. 1.3. Percentage of men (▨) and women (□) in the community who admitted having seen a doctor about abdominal complaints, the subjects being grouped by the number of IBS symptoms revealed by a questionnaire (Heaton et al*, unpublished data)*

The seeking of health care

It has been proposed that patients with IBS have excessive care-seeking behaviour. The data for this are rather scanty. In one study, people who admitted to symptoms of IBS during a ten-minute telephone interview also admitted to more indices of illness behaviour, like seeing a doctor with every sore throat (Whitehead *et al*, 1982). However, this study did not distinguish between patients and non-patients. In a weightier study, Sandler *et al* (1984) compared 33 students or young hospital staff who admitted having seen a doctor for IBS with 53 who had symptoms of IBS but who had not consulted doctors, both groups being picked up by a questionnaire survey. The consulters admitted to more non-gastrointestinal symptoms and to more visits to doctors for such symptoms, even after adjustment for the number of symptoms.

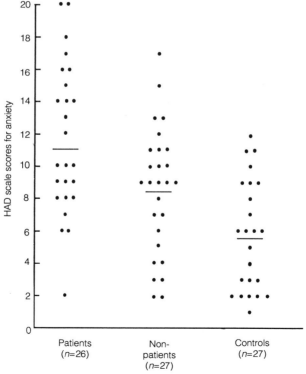

Fig. 1.4. Scores for anxiety in response to the Hospital Anxiety and Depression questionnaire in hospital out-patients with IBS, in non-consulters with IBS ('non-patients') and in pain-denying women of the same age ('controls'). A score of ≥ 11 is considered to be pathological. All differences between groups are statistically significant (Heaton et al, *1991)*

Anxiety

People go to a doctor because they are concerned or worried. This obviously raises the possibility that levels of anxiety are a factor distinguishing patients from non-patients with abdominal pain. We examined this in our prospective study and, as shown in Fig. 1.4, the scores for anxiety were indeed appreciably higher in the patients. Three other studies have compared the psychological state of patients with IBS and non-patients using validated questionnaires (Welch *et al*, 1985; Drossman *et al*, 1988; Whitehead *et al*, 1988). The two largest and most comprehensive ones both showed more psychological distress in the patients (Drossman *et al*, 1988; Whitehead *et al*, 1988). There is little doubt, therefore, that patients are more emotionally disturbed than non-complainers.

Which comes first?

The data do not indicate which comes first – the symptoms or the anxiety. Some of the anxiety may well be the result of the symptoms. Patients constantly tell me that it is; often they fear cancer. If anxiety causes the symptoms, one would expect a correlation between the intensities of each. We found no consistent correlation, except with bloating (Heaton *et al*, 1991). Undoubtedly, stress can alter intestinal motility, and the effect of emotions on the gut are embodied in many everyday expressions like 'gut reaction', 'shit-scared' and 'sickening'. But it is obviously true too that having frequent abdominal pain and disturbed bowel function without understanding what is causing them is stressful and worrying.

Conclusions

Recurrent abdominal pain (mostly intestinal in origin) is experienced by most women and many men. Most people forget about the occasional pain and, of those who remember, most do not consult a doctor. Those who do consult may also have a greater tendency generally to consult doctors and they are certainly more anxious. However, their anxiety may well be due in part to their symptoms, which are worse than those of non-consulters. Several factors interact in leading people with abdominal pain to consult doctors.

References

BI-ZHEN, W. & QI-YING, P. (1988) Functional bowel disorders in apparently healthy Chinese people. *Chinese Journal of Epidemiology*, **9**, 345–349.

BOMMELAER, G., ROUCH, M., DAPOIGNY, M., *et al* (1986) Epidémiologie des troubles functionnels intestinaux dans une population apparemment saine. *Gastroenterologie Clinique et Biologique*, **10**, 7–12.

DROSSMAN, D. A., SANDLER, R. S., MCKEE, D. C., *et al* (1982) Bowel patterns among subjects not seeking health care. Use of a questionnaire to identify a population with bowel dysfunction. *Gastroenterology*, **83**, 529–534.

——, ——, BROOM, C. M., *et al* (1986) Urgency and fecal soiling in people with bowel dysfunction. *Digestive Diseases and Sciences*, **31**, 1221–1225.

——, MCKEE, D. C., SANDLER, R. S., *et al* (1988) Psychosocial factors in the irritable bowel syndrome. A multivariate study of patients and nonpatients with irritable bowel syndrome. *Gastroenterology*, **95**, 701–708.

HEATON, K. W., GHOSH, S. & BRADDON, F. E. M. (1991) How bad are the symptoms and bowel dysfunction of patients with irritable bowel syndrome. A prospective, controlled study with special reference to stool form. *Gut*, **32**, 73–79.

JOHNSEN, R., JACOBSEN, B. K. & FØRDE, O. H. (1986) Associations between symptoms of irritable colon and psychological and social conditions and lifestyle. *British Medical Journal*, **292**, 1633–1635.

O'DONNELL, L. J., HEATON, K. W., MOUNTFORD, R. A., *et al* (1990) Prevalence of the irritable bowel syndrome in a random sample of the British population. *Gut*, **31**, A1173.

SANDLER, R. S., DROSSMAN, D. A., NATHAN, H. P., *et al* (1984) Symptom complaints and health care seeking behavior in subjects with bowel dysfunction. *Gastroenterology*, **87**, 314–318.

THOMPSON, W. G. & HEATON, K. W. (1980) Functional bowel disorders in apparently healthy people. *Gastroenterology*, **79**, 283–288.

WELCH, G. W., HILLMAN, L. C. & POMARE, E. W. (1985) Psychoneurotic symptomatology in the irritable bowel syndrome: a study of reporters and non-reporters. *British Medical Journal*, **291**, 1382–1384.

WHITEHEAD, W. E., WINGET, C., FEDORAVICIUS, A. S., *et al* (1982) Learned illness behavior in patients with irritable bowel syndrome and peptic ulcer. *Digestive Diseases and Sciences*, **27**, 202–208.

——, BOSMAJIAN, L., ZONDERMAN, A. B., *et al* (1988) Symptoms of psychologic distress associated with irritable bowel syndrome. Comparison of community and medical clinic samples. *Gastroenterology*, **95**, 709–714.

2 Relationship of non-organic abdominal pain to psychiatric disorder and life stress

FRANCIS CREED

Several studies have shown that approximately one-third of patients attending a gastroenterology clinic do not have organic disorders (Harvey *et al*, 1983; Holmes *et al*, 1987). From figures used by a working party of the Royal College of Physicians, it can be calculated that between 600 and 1000 new out-patients with non-organic disorders are seen by gastroenterologists in the UK each week (Royal College of Physicians, 1984).

Most patients with non-organic complaints respond reasonably well to routine medical treatment, but a number become persistent complainers and may be intensively and repeatedly investigated. The study of Kingham & Dawson (1985) reported 22 patients with chronic upper abdominal pain, which could be reproduced by distension of the colon with a balloon. These 22 patients had seen a total of 76 consultants. The extensive investigations performed upon them are listed below.

72 pancreatico-biliary procedures	
53 barium X-rays	no abnormality related to symptoms
25 endoscopies	
12 intravenous urograms	

38 operations:	12 appendicectomies	
	10 cholecystectomies	none successful long term
	16 gynaecological or exploratory abdominal operations	

The only investigation which was consistently abnormal was the Hamilton Rating Scale for Depression (four had severe depression, six moderate depression, four mild, and eight were not depressed), a finding which may have been related to the abdominal pain.

9

Two conclusions emerge from this study. Firstly, it is not possible to tell whether the depression is involved in the aetiology of the pain, or whether it results from the persistent and undiagnosed abdominal pain. Secondly, if a gastroenterologist wished to refer these patients for psychiatric assessment or treatment, it is unlikely they would be willing after so many investigations for intra-abdominal pathology. An alternative method of management for such patients is clearly required, other than the never-ending search for organic disease. When the same research group demonstrated how readily non-organic abdominal pain can be reproduced by distension of the colon with a balloon, they wrote "the widespread belief that only the finding of intra-abdominal organic disease is enough to explain a patient's symptoms inhibits the advancement of clinical gastroenterology" (Swarbrick *et al*, 1980).

An alternative model is therefore required. This chapter reviews the evidence that psychological factors contribute to the cause of non-organic abdominal pain. This evidence falls under three headings:

(a) non-organic abdominal symptoms are associated with anxiety/depression
(b) the abdominal pain follows life stress, and is relieved by relief of stress
(c) the abdominal pain is not relieved by physical treatment, but responds to psychological treatment.

Non-organic abdominal pain is associated with psychiatric disorder

Numerous studies have demonstrated that the prevalence of psychiatric disorder, assessed by research criteria, is higher in patients with non-organic abdominal pain or irritable bowel syndrome (IBS) than in those with organic disease (Table 2.1). The prevalence of anxiety/depression is between 40% and 60% in those with non-organic abdominal pain, some two to three times higher than in patients with organic gastrointestinal disease. These studies used standardised clinical interviews, and not self-administered questionnaires, so the results are reliable. The interpretation is, however, difficult. Psychiatric disorder among clinic patients might be a consequence of the abdominal pain, rather than its cause. Only two studies have examined the onset of psychiatric disorder in relation to the onset of abdominal pain (Craig & Brown, 1984; Ford *et al*, 1987). Both found that in the majority of patients with non-organic disorders the psychiatric disorder had preceded the abdominal pain.

The onset of non-organic abdominal pain is associated with life stress

It is necessary first to explain briefly about the assessment of life events in relation to the symptoms. A date for the onset of abdominal pain must be

TABLE 2.1

Prevalence of psychiatric disorder in functional bowel disorder/irritable bowel syndrome using standardised research psychiatric interviews

Author	Number of subjects	Instrument for psychiatric assessment	Functional bowel disorder	Organic gastrointestinal disorder	Healthy controls
McDonald & Bouchier (1980)	32 (FBD[1])	CIS[3]	53%	20%	–
Colgan *et al* (1988)	37 (FBD)	CIS	57%	6%	–
Craig & Brown (1984)	79 (FBD)	PSE[4]	42%	18%	–
Ford *et al* (1987)	48 (IBS[2])	PSE	42%	6%	8%
Toner *et al* (1990)	44 (IBS)	DIS[5]	61%	–	–
Blanchard *et al* (1990)	68 (IBS)	DIS	56%	25	18%
Kingham & Dawson (1985)	22 (FBD)	HRSD[6]	64%	–	–

1. FBD = Functional bowel disorder (i.e. consecutive non-organic gastrointestinal disorders in the clinic).
2. IBS = Irritable bowel syndrome patients.
3. CIS = Clinical Interview Schedule.
4. PSE = Present State Examination.
5. DIS = Diagnostic Interview Schedule.
6. HRSD = Hamilton Rating Scale for Depression.

found. Life events are then systematically assessed for the months before the onset of abdominal pain, *not* before attendance at the clinic. This caveat is important as there are numerous papers that have examined life events before attendance at the clinic, but such research can tell us nothing about the aetiology of the pain.

Control subjects are interviewed in an identical fashion to establish whether the patients have experienced significantly more unfavourable life events. Attention is usually focused on 'severely threatening' events, although the total number of life events can be counted.

The objective threat of each life event is rated on two four-point scales: the immediate (short-term) threat, and the long-term threat – that which remains after one week. A severe event is one which is rated one or two on the four-point scale on both immediate and long-term threat. Severely threatening life events are those which involve bereavement, diagnosis of a life-threatening illness in a close family member, court appearance with a threat of going to prison, marital separation or divorce, or break-up of a longstanding girlfriend/boyfriend relationship. Such events are known to be related to the onset of depression (Brown & Harris, 1978).

In order to assess whether life events precede the onset of non-organic abdominal pain, it is necessary to select patients with a recent onset of pain which can be accurately dated. Fig. 2.1. illustrates three studies. The first was of patients aged 17–30 years undergoing appendicectomy, over one-third of whom had an appendix that, on histological examination, proved not to be acutely inflamed (Creed, 1981). The second study (Craig & Brown, 1984) included patients aged 18–60 years attending a gastroenterology clinic who had a clear onset or recurrence of abdominal pain within one year of the clinic attendance. In each study, patients with organic gastrointestinal illness were used as one control group, and each study also included a comparison group of healthy people.

The assessment of psychiatric disorder and life events was made before it was known whether the patient had an organic diagnosis (such as appendicitis or peptic ulcer) or a 'non-organic' one (appendix not acutely inflamed, or irritable bowel syndrome), so that both patient and researcher were 'blind' to the eventual diagnosis at the time that environmental stress was measured.

The results of another study (Creed *et al*, 1988) are included for comparison because the same measures were used on patients aged 17–35 years who were admitted to hospital following an overdose, since it is well known that these patients have undergone recent crises and become distressed.

Figure 2.1 shows the proportion of subjects who had experienced a severely threatening event during the preceding 38 weeks. This time period is important in the aetiology of depression; it is long enough to include those severe events, such as bereavement, which may affect the individual for some months afterwards, but not so long that distorted data might result from poor recall. Two-thirds of patients with non-organic abdominal pain had experienced such a severe event in the 38 weeks before the onset of their pain (Fig. 2.1.). This proportion is similar to that in patients admitted to hospital with self-poisoning and in patients who develop depressive illness presenting to a psychiatrist.

The commonest severe events are those 'rows' which may herald a marital separation or job loss. These were many times more common in non-organic abdominal pain patients (27%) than the healthy community controls (7%) or patients with organic gastrointestinal disease (6%). They were almost as frequent as in self-poisoning patients (33%).

We examined whether it was only those who had psychiatric disorder who had experienced a severe life event. This was not so – two-thirds of the patients without psychiatric disorder had experienced a severe event before the onset of their abdominal pain (Fig. 2.2).

From these data a provisional model may be developed. A personal crisis may lead directly to abdominal symptoms, perhaps by alteration of colonic motility. The crisis may, in addition, lead to psychiatric disorder, which in turn leads to alteration of colonic function and/or reduction of the subject's threshold to the perception of pain.

Summary

Evidence suggesting that non-organic abdominal symptoms result from psychological disorder has been documented in this chapter. Another convincing line of evidence is the positive response of the symptoms to

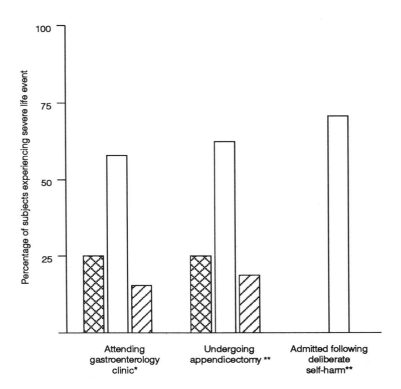

Fig. 2.1. Percentage of subjects who had experienced a severe life event during 38 weeks before onset of abdominal pain or before interview for community comparison group. Organic gastrointestinal disorder/appendicitis (⊠), non-organic abdominal pain (□), community comparison group (⊡). * = P < 0.01, ** = P < 0.0001 compared to community comparison group

psychological treatment when conventional medical treatment has failed. There is now accumulating evidence for the efficacy of psychological treatment for patients with non-organic abdominal pain (Creed & Guthrie, 1989). This is discussed in detail by Dr Guthrie in Chapter 8.

Detection of anxiety, depression and life stress in the clinic

If we are to accept that life stress, and possibly psychiatric disorder, are common in this population, they should be detected at initial assessment. The following questions should enable the doctor to do this with little extra time or alteration of routine clinical practice.

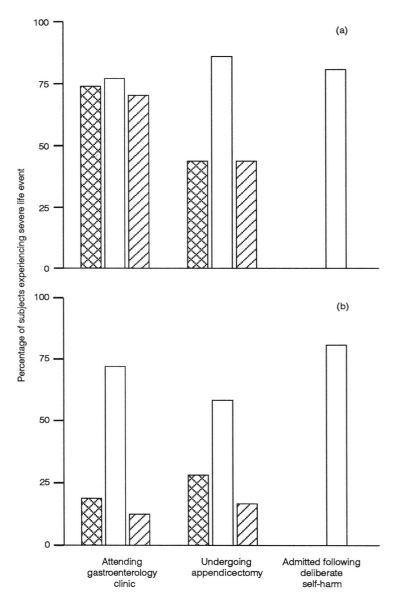

Fig. 2.2. Percentage of subjects (a) with psychiatric illness and (b) without psychiatric illness who had experienced a severe life event during 38 weeks before onset of abdominal pain or before interview for community comparison group. (Organic gastrointestinal disorder/appendicitis (⊠), non-organic abdominal pain (□), community comparison group (▨)).

(a) Exactly when did your (abdominal) symptoms start, or when did this episode start?
(b) When did you last feel quite well?
(c) Does the pain wake you at night – how have you been sleeping recently?
(d) Have you been feeling very worried or anxious for any reason recently?
(e) Have you been feeling depressed or down in the dumps recently?
(f) Have there been important changes or stresses in your life recently?
(g) What do you (the patient) think your symptoms are due to?

Question (a) establishes the date of onset of symptoms, which can later be compared to the date of any stresses (question f). Establishing the date when the patient last felt quite well allows an exploration of all the early symptoms, some of which may have occurred outside the gastrointestinal tract, including symptoms of anxiety and depression. Pain at night is suggestive of a peptic ulcer, but mild pain with marked loss of sleep suggests depression. The patient's belief regarding the origin of the symptoms is crucially important. The doctor may need to treat this belief in order to restore health.

Case report

A 60-year-old lady had suffered abdominal pain for several years. At interview she was not clear about the exact onset but when asked she replied: ''. . . about three years ago . . . I've not been so lively or outgoing as I used to be''. In this way she indicated that her general health had been affected and later admitted to being depressed: ''I've been very tearful, afraid of cancer, and at times I can see no end to it all.''

It became clear later in the interview that her bowel symptoms started around the time that her daughter became severely disabled. The timing is still not exact. However, the patient could recall a symptom-free period of three or four months, two years previously, when her abdominal pain improved. When it became clear that this coincided with a remission in her daughter's illness the patient became distressed declaring, ''I don't want you to think I'm an idiot. I don't see how pain in the bowel has anything to do with the way I feel. [tears] I don't imagine it.''

Conclusion

Evidence has been presented that psychological factors are important in the onset of non-organic abdominal symptoms. It is important that these are identified at initial assessment in the medical out-patient clinic. The case report illustrates the point that not all patients volunteer a link between the onset of non-organic abdominal pain and life stress. The doctor must seek evidence (often non-verbal) of anxiety and/or depression and establish the exacerbation and remission of symptoms in relation to stress or its relief.

The clinical method summarised in this paper will help detect psychological and social problems, usually at the first interview. Such early detection of problems is desirable because this:

(a) may indicate a treatable psychological disorder and/or recent life stress which underlies the abdominal pain
(b) may prevent unnecessary investigations
(c) allows further investigation of psychosocial factors at a later stage if investigations for organic disease prove negative.

References

BLANCHARD, E. B., SCHARFF, L., SCHWARZ, S. P., et al (1990) The role of anxiety and depression in the irritable bowel syndrome. *Behaviour Research and Therapy*, **28**, 401–405.

BROWN, G. W. & HARRIS, T. (1978) *Social Origins of Depression*. London: Tavistock.

COLGAN, S., CREED, F. H., & KLASS, S. H. (1988) Psychiatric disorder and abnormal illness behaviour in patients with upper abdominal pain. *Psychological Medicine*, **18**, 887–892.

CRAIG, T. K. & BROWN, G. W. (1984) Goal frustrating aspects of life event stress in the aetiology of gastrointestinal disorder. *Journal of Psychosomatic Research*, **28**, 411–421.

CREED, F. H. (1981) Life events and appendicectomy. *Lancet*, **i**, 1381–1385.

——, CRAIG, T. & FARMER, R. (1988) Functional abdominal pain, psychiatric illness and life events. *Gut*, **29**, 235–242.

—— & GUTHRIE, E. (1989) Psychological treatment of the irritable bowel syndrome: a review. *Gut*, **30**, 1601–1609.

FORD, M. J., MILLER, R. McC., EASTWOOD, J., et al (1987) Life events, psychiatric illness and the irritable bowel syndrome. *Gut*, **28**, 160–165.

HARVEY, R. F., SALIH, S. Y. & READ, A. E. (1983) Organic and functional disorders in 2000 gastroenterology outpatients. *Lancet*, **i**, 632–634.

HOLMES, K. M., SALTER, R. H., COLE, T. P., et al (1987) A profile of district gastroenterology. *Journal of the Royal College of Physicians*, **21**, 111–114.

KINGHAM, J. G. C. & DAWSON, A. M. (1985) Origins of chronic right upper quadrant pain. *Gut*, **26**, 783–788.

MACDONALD, A. J. & BOUCHIER, P. A. D. (1980) Non-organic gastro-intestinal illness: a medical and psychiatric study. *British Journal of Psychiatry*, **136**, 1276–1283.

ROYAL COLLEGE OF PHYSICIANS (1984) The need for an increased number of consultant physicians with specialist training in gastroenterology. *Gut*, **25**, 99–102.

SWARBRICK, E. T., HEGARTY, J. E., BAT, L., et al (1980) Site of pain from the irritable bowel. *Lancet*, **ii**, 443–446.

TONER, B. B., GARFINKEL, P. E. & JEEJEEBHOY, K. N. (1990) Psychological factors in the irritable bowel syndrome. *Canadian Journal of Psychiatry*, **35**, 158–161.

3 Towards a confident diagnosis of non-cardiac chest pain

JOHN CHAMBERS and CHRISTOPHER BASS

We think of the heart first whenever a person reports chest pain. This is understandable in view of the dangers of failing to diagnose ischaemic disease, but often leads to the mistake of thinking exclusively of the heart and therefore to over-investigation.

As many as 20% of cardiac catheterisations performed for the investigation of chest pain show normal coronary anatomy (NCA). This amounts to at least 12 000 cases in the UK each year. The descriptive label 'chest pain with NCA' which is then applied often perpetuates the implication of cardiac disease. Studies of patients with this diagnosis have maintained the idea of a link between chest pain, however atypical in character, and myocardial ischaemia. Further investigations often include: haemoglobin-oxygen dissociation, myocardial biopsies, coronary sinus lactate extraction, estimates of coronary flow reserve, contrast/radionuclide ventriculography, stress echocardiography, and thallium scans. There is evidence of myocardial ischaemia in a proportion of patients with syndrome X, but this is an uncommon group. For the rest there is no convincing evidence, although an aura of uncertainty is perpetuated by a mass of conflicting results arising partly from technical problems in methods and inexact description of study populations (Chambers & Bass, 1990).

Clinical cardiologists reflect this insecurity about diagnosis because they continue cardiac medications in three-quarters of patients with NCA despite reassuring them that the heart is normal. Thus the patient receives conflicting signals from the doctor and usually no satisfactory explanation for the pain. Three-quarters continue to report pain (Savage *et al*, 1983).

The present cardiac bias in diagnosis is illogical for four reasons:

(a) Chest pain atypical of a cardiac origin is frequent within the community (Table 3.1).
(b) A number of non-cardiac conditions are known to cause or be associated with chest pain. These include oesophageal conditions,

e.g. gastro-oesophageal reflux, nutcracker oesophagus/diffuse spasm; musculoskeletal conditions, e.g. costochondritis, increased tension, osteoarthrosis; psychiatric conditions, e.g. panic, depression, somatisation disorder; and hyperventilation.

(c) Patients with 'chest pain and NCA' have virtually no cardiac morbidity and mortality over ten-year follow-up (Chambers & Bass, 1990). This makes myocardial ischaemia an unlikely origin for the pain.

(d) Even patients proceeding to cardiac catheterisation have pain which is not typical of a cardiac origin. In Day & Sowton's (1976) series, only 16% had pain which was reliably related to exercise. A slightly higher proportion of typical pain was found in an interim analysis of 29 consecutive cases reporting chronic chest pain (Table 3.2), but six cases (21%) never even had exertion-related pain (Chambers *et al*, in preparation).

TABLE 3.1

Frequency of atypical chest pain in the general population and primary care

	n	Study group	Frequency
Savage *et al* (1983)	2717	Relatives of probands with mitral valve prolapse	16%
Hannay (1978)	1344	General practice, Glasgow	7%
von Korff (1988)	1016	Group Health Plan, Seattle	12%

TABLE 3.2

Pain characteristics in 29 cases with chronic chest pain and normal coronary anatomy (Chambers et al, *1991)*

Pain characteristic	n	(%)
On exertion	23	(79)
Reliably on exertion[1]	16	(55)
At rest	23	(79)
>2/10 at rest[2]	17	(59)
Associated breathlessness	21	(72)
Associated gastrointestinal history	14	(48)
Typical[3]	8	(28)

1. In answer to the question "if you went up a steep hill (or some other individually appropriate stressor) on ten separate occasions, on how many would you have chest pain?" (≥7/10 is positive).
2. In answer to the question "if you have ten pains in a row, how many of them occur sitting quietly at rest?"
3. Defined as pain occurring more than six out of ten times on exertion, <3/10 at rest and lasting <20 minutes.

Not surprisingly, the over-zealous search for a cardiac origin for pain produces a poor yield. For example, in a retrospective study of a US Army medical centre, organic abnormalities were found in only 11 of 96 patients presenting with chest pain (Kroenke & Mangelsdorff, 1989). We clearly need the confidence, knowledge and skills to make a positive diagnosis of non-cardiac causes of chest pain.

Moreover, we need to do this quickly and, if possible, without the exhaustive exclusion of coronary disease. The catheter waiting-list may be long enough for patients to develop a fixed lifestyle of invalidity centred on concern about their heart by the time they are given the negative result.

Non-cardiac diagnoses and psychological factors

However, it may be difficult to make a positive non-cardiac diagnosis with certainty. Recent research has broken from a narrow cardiac viewpoint, exploring those non-cardiac mechanisms of pain production for which diagnostic techniques have been developed. Symptoms consistent with hyperventilation occur in about 60% of cases with 'chest pain and NCA' (Bass *et al*, 1983), and hypocapnia measured by end-tidal sampling via a nasal cannula is confirmed in three-quarters of these (Chambers *et al*, 1988). Evidence of oesophageal reflux and spasm or nutcracker oesophagus are also found in about half of all patients with 'chest pain and NCA' (Chambers & Bass, 1990).

Unfortunately, the link between these abnormalities and chest pain is not robust. Voluntary overbreathing at rest reproduces pain in only about half of all cases with symptoms suggesting hyperventilation (Bass *et al*, 1991). In patients with oesophageal reflux or dysmotility, Peters *et al* (1988) found that only 36% of 92 episodes of pain occurred at the same time as an oesophageal abnormality. Furthermore, effective treatment for an observed abnormality does not always relieve chest pain. Despite a dramatic reduction in peristaltic waves in patients with nutcracker oesophagus, nifedipine is no more effective than placebo for improving pain (Richter *et al*, 1987). Longitudinal myotomy, which abolishes all motor activity, has been found to improve pain in only half of cases of oesophageal spasm (Ellis *et al*, 1988).

These studies are limited by the concentration on a single organ or system when it is likely that mechanisms of pain production may overlap and interact. For example, hyperventilation may cause diffuse oesophageal spasm (Rasmussen *et al*, 1986) or it is possible that discomfort from oesophageal reflux may induce hyperventilation. Psychological factors are also likely to be important. Psychological abnormalities occur in between 58% and 70% of patients with chest pain and NCA (Bass & Wade, 1984; Katon *et al*, 1988). Furthermore, the antidepressant trazodone has been shown to be effective against pain in patients with oesophageal abnormalities despite unchanged oesophageal function (Clouse *et al*, 1987).

It is possible that hyperventilation or oesophageal dysfunction may be coincidental findings. The chest pain might be caused by another anxiety-related mechanism such as chest wall cramp. Alternatively, psychological factors might influence the way an abnormal, or even a normal, somatic sensation is perceived and interpreted. For example, one patient may interpret his chest discomfort as indigestion, where another may assume he is having a 'heart attack'. This variation might be explained by a fixed predisposing factor such as personality, which leads to the person constantly worrying about heart disease. But the worry can be precipitated by newspaper articles, television programmes, casual conversations, or the death of a friend from heart disease. Thus a man may ignore his indigestion one day, but after reading an article in the *Times* the next day, may wonder if he has heart disease.

Towards a confident diagnosis of non-cardiac chest pain

How does an assessment of psychological and social factors allow us to establish a diagnosis of non-cardiac chest pain? It should, of course, be part of a comprehensive consideration of both current physical and psychosocial factors and of relevant past history. Cardiac risk factors (family history, hypertension, cigarette smoking, and high serum cholesterol) must be taken into account, as should the age and sex of the patient. In the absence of cardiac risk factors, positive evidence of psychological and social abnormalities assume more significance, especially if the patient is female and under 45 years of age.

Chest pain characteristics

The characteristics of the chest pain must be carefully elicited. Interviewing styles should be flexible, and repeated closed, leading questions should be avoided. For example, instead of asking whether chest pain occurs on exertion, it is more useful to establish the consistency of the relationship between the pain and the exertion, as in this example: "if you were to run upstairs on ten occasions, how often would you experience pain?" Using this criterion, chest pain that occurs at least seven times out of ten is likely to be ischaemic in origin. It should also be established how often the chest pain occurs at rest, and whether it occurs in particular situations, e.g. crowds or lifts (see later). For example, chest pain that is *consistently* related to physical exertion, occurs infrequently at rest, i.e. less than three of the last ten pain episodes, and lasts less than 20 minutes, is more likely to be 'typical' of angina pectoris.

Associated symptoms

Cardiologists routinely ask about chest pain and palpitations, but inquiry about non-cardiac somatic symptoms is also important, especially as other non-organic syndromes such as chronic fatigue and irritable bowel syndrome commonly coexist with atypical chest pain (Kirmayer & Robbins, 1991). The presence of symptoms such as breathlessness, fatigue (especially avoidance of exertion for fear of provoking fatigue), dizziness and paraesthesia make a non-cardiac cause more likely. The interview should not be regarded as complete until these additional symptoms have been sought. It is also important to explore the consequences of the chest pain episodes, and to ask whether the patient is avoiding certain activities (see below).

Is there a psychiatric disorder?

The presence of other somatic (and psychological) symptoms may point to an anxiety disorder. In some patients, discrete episodes of panic may occur, usually because the patient is concerned that the symptoms will lead to a heart attack or sudden death. Such catastrophic thinking is common in panic attacks, therefore it is important to elicit the patient's ideas about aetiology. This may reveal fears of heart disease and death, or a strong conviction of heart disease despite evidence to the contrary.

A psychiatric aetiology is also suggested if there is a situational (or phobic) component to the somatic symptoms. For example, anxiety and panic are common in certain situations such as crowds, public transport, queues, and lifts. Fear of experiencing symptoms in these situations leads to avoidance of them and considerable limitation of activities may occur. Somatic symptoms and a sense of fear generally occur together. Thus the patient who describes having to leave a supermarket because of chest tightness and suffocation is more likely to have a non-cardiac disorder than angina (Beitman *et al*, 1989).

Chest pain also occurs in depressive illness, which may coexist with anxiety and panic. Symptoms include diurnal variation, poor concentration, irritability, low mood, poor appetite with weight loss, and insomnia.

Abnormal psychological processes and pathophysiological mechanisms

Many patients with functional cardiac disorder do not have conspicuous psychiatric disorders (Beitman *et al*, 1990). In such circumstances there may be evidence of abnormal attitudes and beliefs: these include exaggerated fears of death, marked conviction of disease despite negative findings, and intense bodily preoccupation. These abnormal illness beliefs and worries can act as maintaining factors in patients with non-cardiac pain whatever the initial aetiology.

Pathophysiological mechanisms such as hyperventilation can also contribute to symptoms (Gardner *et al*, 1986). It is surprisingly easy to provoke cardiorespiratory symptoms in these patients by using a number of simple provocation tests. The simplest are (a) a breath-holding test, and (b) a hyperventilation provocation test, i.e. asking the patient to overbreathe for 60 seconds. Both exercises may provoke chest discomfort and other familiar somatic symptoms (Chambers *et al*, 1988). These may then be discussed with the patient in terms of what happens during 'stress' and explained as excessive use of, and inability to relax, the respiratory muscles. Previously stoical, resourceful and non-complaining individuals may report fatigue, chest pains and easily provoked breathlessness during or after such procedures.

Physical signs should be actively sought because they are more common in psychological disorders than cardiac disease. These signs, if present, usually indicate some degree of physiological arousal involving the respiratory system. The important physical signs in non-cardiac chest pain are:

(a) obvious sighs and gasping respirations involving assessory muscles of neck
(b) respiratory 'tics' e.g. throat clearing
(c) inability to lie flat without bringing on gasping and chest tightness (this sign has important diagnostic power, provided the patient does not have pulmonary oedema)
(d) short breath-holding time (less than 20 seconds at peak inspiration) (the effort of breath-holding may provoke extreme breathlessness and, sometimes, the patient's usual non-cardiac pain)
(e) localised (one-finger) or diffuse areas of chest wall tenderness.

Stressful life events

A substantial amount of research has attested to the importance of distressing life events as precipitants of anxiety and depressive disorders (Harris, 1989). Despite this, questions about distressing life events before the onset of the symptoms are not routinely sought by physicians. Events signifying loss, threat, and rejection are of particular importance, and are relatively easy to inquire after. Again, open questions are useful, for example "tell me about any changes or setbacks that occurred in the months before your symptoms began".

A longitudinal perspective

Patients with current non-organic chest symptoms may have experienced previous episodes of 'functional' complaints at times of life crisis or stress.

These may have been cardio-respiratory in nature, or any of the other many forms of non-specific complaints such as abdominal pain, and headache. It is particularly important, therefore, to take a longitudinal rather than a cross-sectional perspective when interviewing these patients. This involves inquiring about previous illness episodes, eliciting their relation to life events, and asking about their consequences: What were the symptoms? What tests were performed? What were the results? What was the patient told?

Does it matter if psychological problems are missed?

The answer to this question is a resounding yes, for two main reasons.

(a) Many patients are not reassured by negative tests. For example, Channer *et al* (1987) found that 71% of patients continued to experience chest pain after a negative exercise test, and in two-thirds of these, the pain was sufficient to interfere with normal living. Predictably, patients with persistent pain had significantly higher anxiety and depression scores at presentation. Similarly, patients who undergo subsequent angiography which reveals normal arteries have high rates of continued morbidity: three-quarters continue to report pain and about half remain disabled (Chambers & Bass, 1990). Thus, reassurance alone without an adequate explanation for the cause of the pain is unsatisfactory in over half of investigated patients.

(b) Diagnostic strategies which focus solely on organic causes are extremely costly. In a study in which an organic diagnosis was established in only 11% of primary-care patients presenting with chest pain (Kroenke & Mangelsdorff, 1989), the estimated cost of establishing an organic diagnosis in each of these patients was US $4354.

For these reasons, it is important to establish an early diagnosis of non-cardiac chest pain. This would have major beneficial effects for patients, including: (a) fewer unnecessary investigations; (b) less distress and disability; (c) reduced cost to the hospital; (d) fewer iatrogenic complications.

References

BASS, C., WADE, C., HAND, D., *et al* (1983) Patients with angina with normal and near normal coronary arteries: clinical and psychosocial state 12 months after angiography. *British Medical Journal*, **287**, 1505–1508.
—— & —— (1984) Chest pain with normal coronary arteries: a comparative study of psychiatric and social morbidity. *Psychological Medicine*, **14**, 51–61.
——, CHAMBERS, J. B. & GARDNER, W. N. (1991) Hyperventilation provocation in patients with chest pain and negative treadmill exercise tests. *Journal of Psychosomatic Research*, **35**, 83–89.
BEITMAN, B. D., MUKERJI, V., LAMBERTI, J. M., *et al* (1989) Panic disorder in patients with chest pain and angiographically normal coronary arteries. *American Journal of Medicine*, **63**, 1399–1403.
——, KUSHNER, M., LAMBERTI, J. W., *et al* (1990) Panic disorder without fear in patients with angiographically normal coronary arteries. *Journal of Nervous and Mental Disease*, **178**, 307–312.

CHAMBERS, J. B., KIFF, P., GARDNER, W. N., *et al* (1988) Measurement of end-tidal partial pressure of carbon dioxide increases the diagnostic power of treadmill exercise testing. *British Medical Journal*, **296**, 1281–1285.
—— & BASS, C. (1990) Chest pain and normal coronary anatomy: review of natural history and possible aetiologic factors. *Progress in Cardiovascular Disease*, **33**, 161–184.
CHANNER, K. S., JAMES, M. A., PAPOUCHADO, M., *et al* (1987) Failure of a negative exercise test to reassure patients with chest pain. *Quarterly Journal of Medicine*, **63**, 315–322.
CLOUSE, R. E., LUSTMAN, P. J., ECKERT, T. C., *et al* (1987) Low-dose trazodone for symptomatic patients with esophageal contraction abnormalities: a double-blind, placebo controlled trial. *Gastroenterology*, **92**, 1027–1036.
DAY, L. J. & SOWTON, E. (1976) Clinical features and follow-up of patients with angina and normal coronary arteries. *Lancet*, **ii**, 334–337.
ELLIS, F. H., CROZIER, R. E. & SHEA, J. A. (1988) Long oesophagomyotomy for diffuse oesophageal spasm and related disorders. In *Diseases of the Oesophagus: Pathophysiology, Diagnosis, Conservative and Surgical Treatment* (eds J. R. Siewert & A. H. Holscher), pp. 913–917. Berlin: Springer-Verlag.
GARDNER, W. N., MEAH, M. & BASS, C. (1986) Controlled study of respiratory responses during prolonged measurement in patients with chronic hyperventilation. *Lancet*, **ii**, 826–830.
HANNAY, D. R. (1978) Symptom prevalence in the community. *Journal of the Royal College of General Practitioners*, **28**, 492–499.
Harris, T. O. (1989) Physical illness. In *Life Events and Illness* (eds G. W. Brown & T. O. Harris). London: Unwin Hyman.
KATON, W., HALL, M. L., RUSSO, J., *et al* (1988) Chest pain: relationship of psychiatric illness to coronary angiographic results. *American Journal of Medicine*, **84**, 1–8.
KIRMAYER, L. J. & ROBBINS, J. M. (1991) Functional somatic symptoms. In *Current Concepts of Somatization: Research and Clinical Perspectives* (eds L. J. Kirmayer & J. M. Robbins). Washington, DC: American Psychiatric Press.
KROENKE, K. & MANGELSDORFF, D. (1989) Common symptoms in ambulatory care: incidence, evaluation, therapy and outcome. *American Journal of Medicine*, **86**, 262–266.
PETERS, L., MAAS, L., PETTY, D., *et al* (1988) Spontaneous non-cardiac chest pain: evaluation by 24-hour ambulatory oesophageal motility and pH monitoring. *Gastroenterology*, **94**, 878–886.
RASMUSSEN, K., RAVNBAEK, J., FUNCH-JENSEN, P., *et al* (1986) Oesophageal spasm in patients with coronary artery spasm. *Lancet*, **i**, 174–176.
RICHTER, J. E., DALTON, C. B., BRADLEY, L. A., *et al* (1987) Oral nifedipine in the treatment of non-cardiac chest pain in patients with the nutcracker oesophagus. *Gastroenterology*, **93**, 21–28.
SAVAGE, D. D., DEVEREUX, R. B., GARRISON, R. J., *et al* (1983) Mitral valve prolapse in the general population. 2. Clinical features: the Framingham study. *American Heart Journal*, **106**, 577–581.
VON KORFF, M., DWORKIN, S. F., LE ROSCHE, L., *et al* (1988) An epidemiologic comparison of chest pain complaints. *Pain*, **32**, 173–183.

4 Patients' fears of illness: chest pain and palpitations

RICHARD MAYOU

Chest pain and palpitations are frequently reported in the general population, and are often transient. Non-cardiac atypical chest pain is frequent in all medical settings (Mayou, 1989). As described in the previous chapter, most research has been concerned with patients having normal coronary angiograms who have an excellent medical prognosis with regard to their heart, but who are likely to suffer continuing symptoms and disability, and to continue to consult their doctors about chest pain and related symptoms. Those who are referred for coronary angiography are a highly selected population, and much greater numbers of patients are seen in out-patient clinics, emergency departments and especially in general practice. In each of these settings, many patients with chest pain are not given a diagnosis of heart disease or other physical condition, and reassurance is often ineffective. Less is known about the presenting complaint of palpitations, although it is almost as frequent as chest pain at cardiac clinics. Again, many patients are told there is no medically significant cause.

Examination and simple investigation are often effective in reassuring those with non-cardiac pain and palpitations, especially in general practice. However, the outcome is less good for those attending cardiac clinics, and particularly poor for those who have negative coronary angiograms (Table 4.1). This chapter is mainly concerned with the important minority of patients who are not reassured by negative findings or by straightforward explanation.

The aetiology of chest pain and associated symptoms has been disputed for over 150 years (Mayou, 1989). In a remarkable series of three Goulstonian lectures delivered to The Royal College of Physicians in 1940 and published the next year, Dr Paul Wood described a series of cardiological and clinical investigations on soldiers admitted to a military hospital for effort syndrome. He outlined a multicausal interactive aetiological model for what he renamed Da Costa's syndrome (Wood, 1941). I believe this approach remains fundamental to understanding medically unexplained chest pain,

TABLE 4.1
*Chest pain with normal coronary arteries: outcome at a mean of 6.3 years
for 1244 subjects (adapted from Papanicolau et al, 1986)*

Outcome	%
Continuing chest discomfort	70
Limitation of physical activity	51
Impaired work	19
Cardiac-related admission in last year	13
Anti-anginal medication	27

palpitations, breathlessness and other symptoms. Paul Wood's papers emphasise:

(a) the significance of relatively minor physical problems
(b) the ways in which these are understood by patients.

While describing and emphasising the importance of chest wall pain, hyperventilation, oesophageal sensations and other physical causes, he also stressed the importance of psychological factors. He wrote that

"the reaction becomes linked to effort by a variety of devices, which includes misinterpretation of emotional symptoms, certain vicious circular patterns, the growth of the conviction that the heart is to blame, consequent fear of sudden death on exertion".

Re-reading these lectures, it is interesting how Paul Wood provides a much more informative psychological understanding of aetiology than the companion paper by his psychiatric colleagues, two of the best-known psychiatrists of our time, Sir Aubrey Lewis and Dr Maxwell Jones (Jones & Lewis, 1941). They concentrated on primary psychiatric disorder, whereas Wood emphasised much wider psychological factors.

It is important that we should do the same today. We must, as Chambers & Bass emphasise in the previous chapter, avoid preoccupation with single explanations of atypical chest pain, and accept that it is common for aetiology to be multicausal with an interaction between physical, psychological and social variables. Emphasis on the psychological and social contributions to symptoms is not the same as saying that traditional psychiatric disorder is the explanation. Clinicians are more concerned with ordinary people, who for reasons which are often entirely understandable and reasonable, misinterpret symptoms as being more threatening and disabling than is medically justified. Only a proportion are suffering from anxiety and depressive disorders, and although the multisymptomatic 'thick file' chronic patients are an important, conspicuous and demanding group, they are a very small minority.

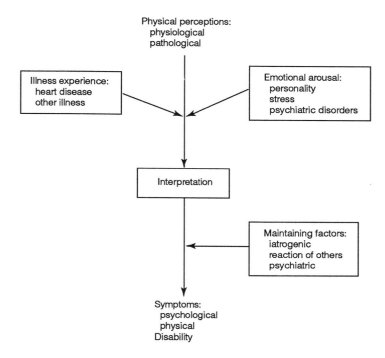

Fig. 4.1. An aetiological model for non-cardiac atypical chest pain

An aetiological model

Figure 4.1 shows a simple version of the model. It is basically the same model as that used implicitly in other chapters and by Wood, although in the absence of any agreed terminology we differ in emphasis and in the words we use.

The central feature of the model is the concept that subjective symptoms, physical and psychological, are the result of patients' interpretation (or attribution) of somatic perceptions. These underlying perceptions may be due to minor physical pathology, excessive awareness of normal physical and bodily processes, or to hyperventilation. They may also be due to the somatic consequences of anxiety or other primary psychiatric disorder.

Most of the time we correctly interpret such bodily perceptions as due to physical causes or stress, but sometimes we are uncertain, and sometimes we make erroneous assumptions. There are many psychosocial variables which make it more likely that individuals will misinterpret their bodily perceptions as more threatening than is in fact the case. They can be grouped into longstanding predisposing and acute precipitating factors. Once established, these same or other factors may then maintain the misinterpretation. Two broad groups of predisposing and precipitating factors are prominent: (a) illness knowledge and experience; (b) emotional arousal.

(a) Illness knowledge and experience – This first group includes knowledge of heart disease and other illnesses, family history of heart disease, models of heart disease in friends and neighbours, general experience of doctors, and satisfaction with medical care. Unsurprisingly, atypical non-cardiac chest pain, palpitations, and breathlessness are very common in those with undoubted heart disease. Those recovering from infarction or cardiac surgery frequently worry about medically insignificant aches and pains.

(b) Emotional arousal – The second group of predisposing and precipitating factors are those resulting from the interaction between personality and stress, grouped in Fig. 4.1 under the heading of emotional arousal. This term covers concern, worry and autonomic arousal which are more common than diagnosable psychiatric disorders. However, the latter are common and include:

(i) anxiety disorder, with or without panic attacks
(ii) major depressive illness, in which profound pessimism distorts views of the past, present and future
(iii) the rather poorly defined disorders which modern psychiatric classifications group together as somatoform disorder (i.e. hypochondriasis and other syndromes in which the most prominent feature is persistent concern about physical symptoms despite full medical investigation and reassurance).

Once symptoms are established, they may be maintained or reinforced by the patient's persistent awareness of the minor physical perceptions, or by other factors, such as secondary anxiety and panic, the reactions of friends and relatives, the reactions and actions of doctors. Each of these factors may lead a patient who has suffered temporary chest discomfort to experience prolonged over-concern. Our own medical uncertainty about diagnosis can powerfully reinforce the anxious patient's worries. Thus, doctors often reassure that chest pain is of no clinical importance, but then prescribe nitrates, or speak obscurely about 'floppy valves'.

This model is wide ranging. It covers heterogeneous clinical problems. It covers those with major psychiatric disorder. It also explains the aetiology of worry about heart disease by the middle-aged man who has ignored minor indigestion until his twin brother died of a heart attack. This, not unreasonably, focuses his attention and concern on his symptoms and may precipitate autonomic symptoms of anxiety and hyperventilation. His doctor's caution may increase the uncertainty.

The multicausal interactive model helps us to understand aetiology by stressing minor physical problems and also individual beliefs, personality and circumstances. It also points to ways in which medical intervention could reduce distress and disability by modifying the patient's interpretations of his symptoms. We cannot rely solely on reassuring him that there is no serious physical cause, since as we have seen, this is often ineffective. There is considerable scope for reducing contradictions and ambiguities, but routine management must always include an explanation and appropriate advice. Sometimes the misinterpretations are so persistently and firmly held that there is a need for intensive specialist treatments which aim specifically to modify physical and psychological factors. These include the use of antidepressant drugs (Chapter 10) and the psychological (so-called cognitive–behavioural) approach (Chapter 9).

A study of cardiac clinic attenders

To illustrate and justify the interactive model for patients presenting with chest pain and palpitations, I shall take the example of our own experience from 94 consecutive attenders at an Oxford cardiac clinic with the presenting symptoms of chest pain or palpitations. The cardiologists completed a research assessment sheet at the end of the consultation. We then briefly interviewed the patients, and asked them to complete self-report scales. We reassessed patients at six months, by interviewing them at home, and again at three years by postal and telephone questionnaires.

Overall, 62% of this sample were diagnosed by the cardiologists as not having heart disease or any other serious physical cause of their symptoms, and were reassured and usually discharged back to general practitioner (GP) care. It is my impression that this proportion would be similar in most other cardiac clinics.

What happened to these people? When interviewed six months later, a minority said that they were fit and without symptoms, but the majority still had symptoms, did not feel reassured and described effects on everyday life (see Table 4.2). Many were dissatisfied with medical care, especially in general practice, and much less satisfied than other patients in the consecutive series who were diagnosed as having heart disease. This poor outcome changed little during the following two and a half years. At the final, three-year review, 70% reported they had suffered symptoms in the last three months, symptoms which were frequently described as severe, and moderately or very distressing. There was no overall improvement in mood, and 65% had attended their GPs in the previous three months, although none were currently attending out-patient clinics.

What can we say about the characteristics of these patients in terms of the model already outlined? Table 4.3 summarises the findings for those

TABLE 4.2
Consecutive referrals to a cardiac clinic: outcome of 'non-cardiac'
group (62%) at six months

Outcome	%
Improved (self-report)	59
Symptoms in last month	76
Limitation of activity	20
Effect on work	26
Effect on walking	24
Reassured	
no	39
partially	46

TABLE 4.3
Characteristics of new patients referred to a cardiac clinic with presenting symptoms of
chest pain or palpitations and assessed as 'non-cardiac' (%)

Cardiologists' assessment	Chest pain	Palpitations
Physical factors		
chest wall	33	—
oesophagus	10	—
other	15	—
not known	42	—
awareness of tachycardia	—	33
awareness of ectopics	—	67
Hyperventilation	21	33
Psychiatric consultation	30	39
History		
previous consultation for	15	56
'nerves'		
model for heart disease	26	11
(in relatives or others)		
cardiac drugs	41	33
cardiac diagnosis	18	—
Research ratings		
psychiatric disorder	38	50

with non-cardiac chest pain and those with benign palpitations. Let us look
first of all at those with non-cardiac chest pain. The cardiologists' ratings
showed that they used an implicit multicausal model of non-cardiac chest
pain. They frequently diagnosed minor physical factors as having been, or
continuing to be, significant. In addition, they separately rated
hyperventilation and psychiatric factors as contributing causes, and often
noted other non-specific physical complaints. These are the same factors
discussed by Wood (1941). There was also considerable evidence in the
patients' previous histories of two groups of predisposing factors. Awareness
of heart disease in families and friends was frequent. A high proportion
reported previous consultation for their 'nerves'; some had longstanding
psychological problems. Psychiatric disorder was more common than in the

general population. We rated one-third as suffering from psychiatric disorder, either anxiety or depression. Some described panic attacks. Maintaining and reinforcing factors were often obvious. A number of patients had been taking cardiac drugs before referral, some had been told that they had heart disease, a number had previously attended emergency departments and out-patient clinics for chest pain.

The general picture for the smaller number of patients who presented with palpitations is similar. The cardiologists thought that all patients were "excessively aware" of their cardiac rhythm, either tachycardia or occasional ventricular ectopics. Predisposing, precipitating and maintaining factors were similar to those for non-cardiac chest pain. Panic attacks were commonly diagnosed at psychiatric assessment.

Although our cardiologists were implicitly using a multicausal interactive model in their assessment, and made considerable efforts to explain and reassure, they were frequently unsuccessful in allaying concern. It appears they were not able to deal with patients' fears and worries. We asked our patients at three-year follow-up what they thought had been the causes of their chest pain or palpitations. A quarter still believed they had heart disease. A wide range of other physical causes were also mentioned, including problems in the chest wall and gastrointestinal disorders; less often the menopause, caffeine, and virus infections were mentioned. Over half said that stress was the cause or a contributing factor. A quarter did not know the cause, a reply that sometimes indicated acceptance and sometimes continuing fear of a sinister explanation.

It was evident that although some patients with persistent symptoms were still concerned about heart disease, most were not, but they had (or had had) other significant concerns. This research, other research evidence, and clinical experience all indicate that although continuous or intermittent concern about heart disease is prominent in patients with atypical pain or palpitations, it is not the only type of distressing fear. Many patients say they fully accept the cardiologist's explanation, but what they are worried about is the lack of any alternative explanation for continuing symptoms. They say: "my pain is so bad that there must be a serious cause" and complain that doctors are not taking this seriously. Such patients are often not enthusiastic about unheralded blunt assertions that stress is responsible for their pain and they resist suggestions they should see a psychiatrist.

A controlled trial of psychological treatment

Our out-patient study, and some similar evidence from other sources (normal coronary angiograms, emergency departments, general practice), is consistent with the proposed aetiological model, but not conclusive. A final, and perhaps the most convincing, argument for an interactive aetiology is evidence that treatments derived from the model can be effective. There has been considerable clinical experience, a few descriptive reports and a very few systematic evaluations.

Treatment of the underlying physical pathology can be helpful. There is some evidence that drug treatment of those with associated panic disorder is also effective (Beitman *et al*, 1988). We know also that a small number of patients suffer from a major depressive illness for which antidepressants are helpful.

There is increasing evidence that psychological interventions can be effective in changing beliefs and interpretations (attributions) and in improving symptoms and disability. Paul Wood put this succinctly fifty years ago:

> "Simple reassurance and some superficial explanation are quite inadequate. The patient must feel that at last he has met a doctor who thoroughly understands his case. . . . Adequate explanation must follow and will vary according to the chief symptoms. The object is to convince the patient that symptoms are emotionally produced. . . . Once he appreciates the fact that if he no longer fears his symptoms, he will cease to aggravate them, the point is scored." (Wood, 1986 (3rd edn))

It is probable that many more patients could be reassured in general practice or in out-patient clinics by straightforward efforts to understand their beliefs and worries, to discuss them and to offer alternative explanations. Patients need to feel that the doctors accept the reality of their symptoms, and are frequently relieved to know they have a common, explicable and treatable problem. Explanation in terms of nervous tension is more acceptable than abrupt mention of possible psychiatric disorder.

A modern specialist version of this approach is so-called 'cognitive-behavioural' treatment which has proven successful in treating anxiety disorders (Clark, 1986). We recently evaluated an adaptation of this approach in a controlled trial of patients whose non-cardiac chest pain had persisted, despite negative investigations, and who had been referred to us by GPs (Pearce *et al*, 1990; Klimes *et al*, 1990). Subjects were allocated to treatment or to assessment only, and were reassessed at the end of the treatment or after three months.

The control group was unchanged at follow-up, but there was significant improvement in the frequency of episodes of chest pain in the treatment group. One-third of treated subjects were completely free of symptoms and a further half reported marked reduction in frequency of chest pain. There were also statistically significant advantages for psychological treatment over 'assessment only' on measures of limitation of activities and mood, together with improvements in associated physical symptoms, such as palpitations, breathlessness and fatigue. Use of cardiac and psychotropic drugs was much reduced. Improvements were maintained at review three months later.

As this encouraging outcome was observed in patients with chronic complaints in whom clinical GP care had failed, it might be expected that similar psychological benefit at an earlier stage of medical care would be even more successful.

Conclusion

Non-cardiac chest pains, palpitations, and breathlessness are common in all medical settings: general practice, emergency departments, out-patient clinics and in-patient departments. Only a proportion of patients, especially hospital attenders, are reassured by negative investigations and direct reassurance. This is a major clinical problem. Many patients are suffering prolonged and substantial distress, and their management absorbs considerable medical resources. There is a need to define more effective management and to make it widely available in the simplest possible form.

I have reviewed the evidence for a multicausal interactive model, and argued that it has practical implications. We now need to consider how we can improve the delivery of treatment so that we can provide efficient, effective care for large numbers of people in all medical settings. Some of them have relatively simple needs, and some require specialist intervention. This is principally a question for general practitioners and physicians who must accept the main clinical responsibility. It is also a question for psychiatrists who must be willing to acquire the expertise to offer specialist support and services. Physicians and psychiatrists should collaborate to develop and evaluate treatments suitable for general practice and hospital care.

References

BEITMAN, B. D., BASHA, I. M., TROMBKA, L. H., *et al* (1988) Alprazolam in the treatment of cardiology patients with atypical chest pain and panic disorder. *Journal of Clinical Psychopharmacology*, **8**, 127–130.

CLARK, D. M. (1986) A cognitive approach to panic. *Behavioural Research and Therapy*, **24**, 461–470.

JONES, M. & LEWIS, A. (1941) Effort syndrome. *Lancet*, 813–818.

KLIMES, I., MAYOU, R. A., PEARCE, M. J., *et al* (1990) Psychological treatment for atypical non-cardiac chest pain: a controlled evaluation. *Psychological Medicine*, **20**, 605–611.

MAYOU, R. A. (1989) Invited review: atypical chest pain. *Journal of Psychosomatic Research*, **33**, 373–406.

PAPANICOLAU, M. N., CALIFF, R. M., HIATKY, M. A., *et al* (1986) Prognostic implications of angiographically normal and insignificantly narrower coronary arteries. *American Journal of Cardiology*, **58**, 1181–1187.

PEARCE, M. J., MAYOU, R. A. & KLIMES, I. (1990) The management of atypical non-cardiac chest pain. *Quarterly Journal of Medicine*, **281**, 991–996.

WOOD, P. (1941) Da Costa's syndrome (or effort syndrome). *British Medical Journal*, i, 767–772, 805–811, 845–851.

—— (1986) *Diseases of the Heart and Circulation* (3rd edn). London: Eyre Spottiswood.

5 The management of patients with chronic headache not due to obvious structural disease

ANTHONY HOPKINS

Most of us experience headaches from time to time. The frequent occurrence of advertisements for simple analgesics on television reassures us that self-medication is safe and appropriate, and that rapid relief can be obtained by taking some simple analgesic such as paracetamol, or a non-steroidal anti-inflammatory agent such as ibuprofen. Manufacturers of these drugs probably do not undertake any serious epidemiological research, but a market exists. Epidemiological studies have shown that about 9% of the population have had at least one 'very severe or almost unbearable headache' each year (Newland et al, 1978), and 76% of young women, on inquiry, admit to having had a headache in the previous 28 days (Linet et al, 1989). Fortunately, the lay perception of headache is that it is one of the trials of life to which man (or more particularly woman) is heir, and in most cases a headache is accepted philosophically, without the subject seeking any medical advice.

A proportion of those with headache, however, do consult their general practitioner. The Third National Morbidity Survey undertaken by the Office of Population Censuses and Surveys showed that at least 21 per 1000 population consult their family doctors each year for headache (ICD 791) and migraine (ICD 346) each year (Office of Population Censuses and Surveys, 1986) (Table 5.1). The consultation rate may be even higher, as figures for tension headache (ICD 306.8) are not given in the Third Survey. Table 5.1 also shows the striking gender difference in consultation rate for headache and migraine. Consultation rates are higher for women in each age group. For headaches classified as migrainous, the group consultation rate by women in the age group 45 to 64 is about three and a half times the consultation rate for men.

General practitioners (GPs) cope nobly with most of the large numbers of patients consulting for headaches, but they do refer about 17% for a hospital opinion (Office of Population Censuses and Surveys, 1974). These referrals are in turn a large burden for neurologists. Figure 5.1 shows the

Table 5.1

Patients consulting their family doctor per 1000 population in one year for tension headache (ICD-8, 306.8), headache (ICD 791), and migraine (ICD 346). Data from the Second National Morbidity Survey (Office of Population Censuses and Surveys, 1974); figures in parentheses are from the Third National Morbidity Survey (Office of Population Censuses and Surveys, 1986) (which used ICD-9 criteria, codes 784.0 and 346 for the two respective headings – in this second publication, figures for tension headache are not comparable to those in the first)

	Tension headache	Headache	Migraine
Men: age in years			
15–	3.1	4.2 (11.0)	6.1 (5.8)
25–	4.0	3.6 (10.3)	7.0 (6.2)
45–	3.2	2.7 (8.2)	3.5 (4.9)
65–	1.4	3.0 (8.8)	2.1 (2.8)
75–	0.7	5.2 (8.5)	0.2 (0.9)
All ages	2.7	3.2 (9.4)	4.6 (4.7)
Women: age in years			
15–	9.4	8.2 (23.1)	11.4 (14.3)
25–	11.4	6.4 (21.2)	16.9 (17.6)
45–	6.6	5.5 (15.1)	12.2 (14.1)
65–	3.1	4.2 (13.3)	3.6 (4.7)
75–	2.2	2.7 (13.0)	2.3 (1.7)
All ages	6.5	5.0 (16.7)	9.8 (11.3)
Total	4.7	4.1 (13.2)	7.3 (8.2)

Total number of all ages consulting family doctor about any type of headache (if independent) = 16.1 (>21.4 in 1986).

ICD diagnoses for all patients encountered by 13 neurologists in the United Kingdom in one week in 1986. It can be seen that headache and migraine combined is the most common diagnosis made (Hopkins *et al*, 1989*a*).

These figures show that consultant neurologists will necessarily spend a considerable proportion of their working life in helping patients with headache and migraine. Unfortunately, the amount of training that neurological registrars receive in how to help patients with various neurological illnesses seems to be in inverse proportion to the numbers that they will encounter in subsequent daily practice. No formal training in the management of patients with the common types of headache was given to me as a registrar or senior registrar, perhaps not surprisingly as there is little good research evidence about the cause and the effectiveness of treatment of different types of headache. However, much the same could be said about multiple sclerosis, a disorder which figures prominently in under- and postgraduate training.

Some of those who are interested in research in headache compound the difficulties of the field by writing elaborate classifications which suggest that a careful history and physical examination will somehow so accurately classify a patient's headache that appropriate treatment will follow. Most headache conferences and journals are full of papers about unusual types of headaches such as cluster headache, or about different surgical approaches for the management of intractable trigeminal neuralgia. The body of research in common-or-garden headache is slight, and that which is available is so often

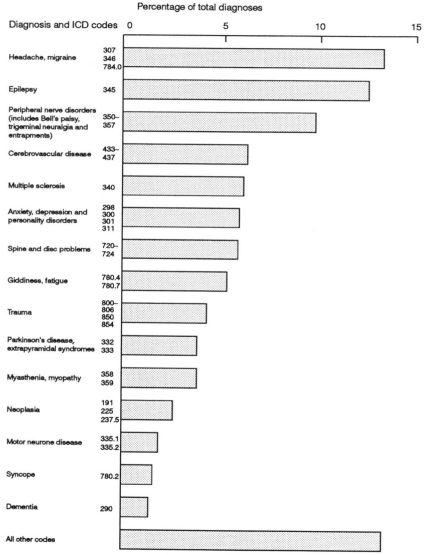

Fig. 5.1. Distribution of diagnoses of 411 new patients seen in one week by 13 neurologists in the UK (from Hopkins et al 1989a; reproduced by permission of the Journal of Neurology, Neurosurgery and Psychiatry)

poorly designed and conducted that few lessons can be drawn. The following extract is from the recent International Classification of Headache (International Headache Society, 1988).

Tension-type headache
1. Episodic tension-type headache
   1.1. Episodic tension-type headache associated with disorder of pericranial muscles
   1.2. Episodic tension-type headache unassociated with disorder of pericranial muscles
2. Chronic tension-type headache
   2.1. Chronic tension-type headache associated with disorder of pericranial muscles
   2.2. Chronic tension-type headache unassociated with disorder of pericranial muscles
3. Headache of the tension-type not fulfilling above criteria.

Those who write such classifications should remember the embarrassment caused to their colleagues interested in motor neurone diseases who spent years classifying the different minor variants of familial spinal muscular atrophy only to find that most appear to be due to a different phenotypic expression of one genotype (Munsat *et al*, 1990). In a recent advertisement for Syndol, a proprietary medication widely advertised, the caption was ''Tension headache, migraine. Whatever you call it – it's bad. But before it takes over, take Syndol''. I must confess to having some sympathy with the rather cavalier attitude to diagnosis expressed. There is sound epidemiological work from Waters (1986) in the UK, from Zeigler *et al* (1982) in the US, and from Drummond & Lance (1984) in Australia to the effect that symptoms commonly attributed to migraine such as teichopsia (scintillating scotomata), unilaterality of headache and vomiting are distributed independently throughout the population; those who have a sufficient number of such symptoms are selected out by physicians and labelled 'classical migraine'. On the other hand, in clinical practice, it is difficult to ignore the reality of an episode of classical migraine so severe that local cerebral blood flow is profoundly reduced (Lauritzen *et al*, 1983), and a hemiplegia occurs.

The patient's view

George Newman wrote 60 years ago that ''There are four questions which in some form or other every patient asks of his doctor: (a) what is the matter with me? This is *diagnosis*. (b) Can you put me right? This is *treatment* and *prognosis*. (c) How did I get it? This is *causation*. (d) How can I avoid it in future? This is *prevention*'' (Newman, 1931). I have no particular quarrel with

TABLE 5.2

Ranking of those factors about the consultation considered most important by 91 patients with headache and 50 doctors (Packard, 1979)

	Doctors: %	Patients: %
Pain relief	96	69
Explanation	68	77
Medication	68	20
Explanation of medication	0	32
Time for questions	68	20
Doctor follow-up	20	26
Neurological examination	6	31
Eye examination	2	11
Alternative treatment to medication	2	18
X-rays	2	8
Possibility of		
psychiatric evaluation	0	3
talking with other patients in a group	0	0

this set of sensible questions, but this framework for patient management is rude and mechanical, as illustrated as follows: "You have migraine (*diagnosis*). You should take ergotamine tartrate (*treatment*). No-one knows the cause, but it often runs in families (*causation*). You may be able to reduce the frequency of some attacks by avoiding cheese, chocolate and red wine (*prevention*)." It would be perfectly possible for a neurologist to manage all the migrainous headaches that he sees along these simplistic lines, and I rather fear that many doctors do. For headache patients at least, Newman's scheme is inadequate. Packard (1979) was one of the first to show the mismatch between what patients with headaches wanted from their neurological consultations, and what the physicians thought they wanted. Some data from Packard's work are presented in Table 5.2. For example, more than three times as many physicians as patients thought that medication was one of the three most important aspects of a consultation for headache. Even in 1979, the year of Packard's publication and before the current explosion of consumer interest in holistic medicine, 18% of headache patients were interested in exploring treatment other than medication, whereas only 2% of physicians were so interested.

Tension headaches and investigations for organic disease

The very name 'tension headache' is a confusing issue. The word 'tension' is used in different ways by different people. Some refer to the patient being 'tense' in the sense of being anxious. However, experienced neurologists meet every week patients whom they diagnose as having tension headache, insofar as there are no features of migraine or other significant illness, and yet the subjects insist that their lives are perfect in every way, and that there are no grounds for psychological tension. Equally, although headache is a common manifestation of a depressive illness (Garvey *et al*, 1983), the occurrence of headaches in patients with symptoms of anxiety severe enough to warrant a psychiatric diagnosis of anxiety disorder are no more frequent than in control subjects (Garvey, 1985).

As to unfavourable life events, few systematic studies exist. Holm *et al* (1986) compared the experience of major adverse life events and everyday 'hassles' in a population of college students with recurrent tension headache, and control students free or nearly free from headache. There was a slight excess of major life events in those with headaches in the year preceding the assessment compared to the control subjects, but a much larger number of 'hassles'. A cognitive evaluation suggested that headache sufferers perceived stressful events as more distressing occurrences than did the control subjects, particularly when the event was such that no control could be exercised over it. There is a danger here. Evidence of adverse life events should not be considered in isolation. All neurologists, rightly in my view, explore the life situation of a patient with chronic recurrent headache, and may then seize upon some presumed adverse life event such as difficulty at work to account for the headache, even though, in this particular instance, there may be a clear-cut organic explanation.

If psychological 'tension' is a rather forced explanation for many patients with 'tension headache', then so is the concept of excessive muscular contraction or muscle tension as a cause of headache. The whole subject is well covered in reviews by Philips & Hunter (1982) and by Pikoff (1984) in the early 1980s. While there is no doubt that under laboratory conditions voluntary sustained contraction of the scalp muscles, aided in some experiments by biofeedback control, will induce headache, other studies show that there is no frontalis electromyogram (EMG) activity during headaches diagnosed as tension headaches. Even when such EMG activity is demonstrated, there is no correlation between EMG activity and clinical improvement. Furthermore, some patients confidently diagnosed as having migraine also have frontalis and temporal muscle EMG activity. It seems therefore that scalp muscle contraction may sometimes occur as a response to pain, and that sometimes there may be an association between muscle contraction and perceived pain, although both may be independently related to an unknown third variable. In the light of these experiments, there is little justification for a detailed classification of tension headache as shown on page 37. The work cited above (Ziegler *et al*, 1982; Drummond & Lance, 1984; Waters, 1986) suggests that apart from cluster headache (migrainous neuralgia), there is no other clear-cut combination of symptoms comprising distinct entities. Drummond & Lance (1984) write that ''classical migraine, common migraine, tension, vascular and tension headache categories are spaced at regular intervals along the common migraine syndrome factor''. It is for this reason that I have suggested a much simpler classification for chronic recurrent headaches (Hopkins, 1988).

(a) Common headache. *Variants/near synonyms:* 'muscle contraction headache', 'tension headache', 'common migraine', 'psychogenic headache', 'recurrent non-specific headache'
    (i) With no obvious cause
    (ii) As a response to an unsatisfactory life situation
    (iii) As a manifestation of a definite depressive illness or anxiety state
    (iv) As a specific anxiety in relation to the presence of cerebral tumour
    (v) Subsequent to trauma
    (vi) In association with cervical spondylosis or after whiplash injuries
    (vii) Induced or exacerbated by oral contraceptives
    (viii) As a result of 'eye-strain' – usually reflecting poor posture and illumination rather than a refractive error
(b) Headache with focal neurological symptoms. *Synonyms:* 'classical migraine' or, if neurological deficit is more substantial, 'hemiplegic', 'ophthalmoplegic' or 'basilar' migraine.
(c) Vascular headache
    (i) Ischaemic vascular disease
    (ii) Carotid dissection
    (iii) Angioma
    (iv) Cluster headache, *synonym:* 'migrainous neuralgia'
    (v) Induced by sudden increases in blood pressure
        with monoamine oxidase inhibitors
        in paraplegia
        with phaeochromocytoma
    (vi) Induced by general cranial vasodilatation
        with CO_2 retention in chronic respiratory failure
        with amyl nitrite, etc.
    (vii) Cranial arteritis, *synonym:* 'temporal arteritis'
(d) Headache in association with raised intracranial pressure
    (i) Primary or metastatic cerebral tumour
    (ii) Subdural haematoma
    (iii) Hydrocephalus
    (iv) Benign intracranial hypertension
    (v) Cough headache
(e) Exertional and coital headache
(f) Cranial neuralgias
(g) Anatomical distortions or variations in the skull and facial bones

Faced with such diagnostic difficulties, it is not surprising that neurologists approach the investigation of headaches in many different ways. My colleagues

TABLE 5.3
Percentage of neurologists who would recommend selected diagnostic procedures for headache (Hopkins et al, *1989b)*

	UK neurologists	US neurologists
No diagnostic tests	62	25
Full blood count	27	43
Urinalysis	19	4
Skull X-ray	19	0
Blood Venereal Disease Research Laboratory test	15	36
Computerised tomography scan	12	54
Chest X-ray	4	0
Smooth-muscle antibody-12	4	39
Electroencephalogram	0	36
Other	0	14
Lumbar puncture	0	7
Duration of voluntary apnoea test	0	0

and I (Hopkins *et al*, 1989*b*) explored such variations in practice among groups of neurologists from the UK and from the US. These neurologists were asked to list the investigations that they would perform upon a patient with the following history.

"A woman of 38 presents with frontal and bi-temporal headaches. These began six weeks before being seen in your clinic, and have recurred two to three times a week since then, each one lasting one to two days. There is no prior or family history of headaches. There are no signs on general or neurological examination."

Table 5.3 shows the very considerable variations in investigations considered necessary for this hypothetical patient. It can be seen that whereas no UK physician thought that an electroencephalogram would contribute to the resolution of the patient's problem, 36% of the US physicians thought that this was an appropriate investigation. Conversely, no US physician thought that a skull X-ray would be useful, whereas 19% of neurologists in the UK specified this as an appropriate investigation. Overall, far more UK than US neurologists were content to leave the patient without any investigations at all.

The sensitivity (detection rate) and specificity (1 – the false-positive rate) of all the investigations listed in Table 5.3 are remarkably low for the elucidation of the cause of a patient's headache. To take computerised tomography (CT) scanning, for example, Larson *et al* (1980) found the sensitivity (detection rate) of CT scanning to be so low that they found no cases of brain tumour among 145 patients referred for headache causing sufficient concern for referral by another physician. With regard to specificity, although false-positive scans suggesting tumours are not frequent, neurologists recognise that unexpected findings unrelated to the cause of headache such as lacunar infarcts or some degree of atrophy are so common that real difficulties arise in explaining the significance of these findings to patients anxious about the cause of their headaches (Hopkins, 1988).

Fears of illness

The anxieties and expectations of a series of patients with common headache attending a number of neurological clinics in and around London have been studied (Fitzpatrick & Hopkins, 1981, 1988; Hopkins, 1989). We found that 60% of 109 patients were concerned about the possibility of organic illness as a cause for their headaches, notably about the possibility of a brain tumour or an impending stroke. The interviewers' ratings, supported by the Present State Examination (Wing *et al*, 1974), suggested that only 18 of the 109 were psychiatrically ill; 12 of these 18 subsequently proved to be taking psychotropic medication. Of greater interest is the psychological normality of the vast majority of those patients concerned about organic illness. Our study showed that it was relatively easy to reassure most patients, and that reassurance was not related to whether the patient had been investigated, nor, interestingly enough, to the seniority of the doctor who had seen the patient. Those who were not reassured were significantly more likely to have been critical of information received at the consultation. Of the 109 patients, 26 were dissatisfied with the information received three weeks after the neurological consultation, particularly in relation to the adequacy of the discussion of what the diagnosis meant to them in terms of their own lives, the likely causation of their headache, how they could avoid headaches in the future, and the likely prognosis. With regard to the more technical aspects of the consultation, only six patients felt that there had been an inadequate physical examination, and only six that investigation had been inadequate.

Analysis of the data suggested that although patients may often have reasons to be dissatisfied with how a neurologist handles their consultation for headache, patient variables are also important. Although age, sex, social class, education, marital status, status of the doctor consulted, the type of hospital (teaching or district) and the degree of investigation and follow-up were not related to patient satisfaction, the following variables were: that the patient him/herself had initiated the referral ($P<0.05$), the patient was rated by the interviewers as anxious or depressed ($P<0.02$), that the headaches had been going on for more than one year ($P<0.01$), and that the neurologist's diagnosis was migraine as opposed to tension headache ($P<0.05$). The patients who were rated as having previously defined their own problem as migraine, and knowing a lot about it – the so-called 'expert sufferers' – were particularly likely to be dissatisfied ($P<0.001$). It is of course such anxious or depressed migraineuses who have had migraine for a long time, who know a lot about the illness, and who themselves initiate referral, who are particularly likely to end up at special clinics for migraine.

TABLE 5.4

Patients' ratings of their headaches one year after neurological consultation (%) (Fitzpatrick & Hopkins, 1988)

	Less severe	Less frequent
Satisfied (n = 57)	67*	74
Dissatisfied (n = 18)	33*	61

*$P < 0.02$.

Henryk-Gutt & Rees (1973) have also shown the different psychological characteristics of those who attend migraine clinic.

Outcomes of the neurological consultation

This book is more about effective management of patients in hospital out-patient departments than of those in special clinics. What outcomes do neurologists achieve after their consultations for headache? In the London study previously cited (Fitzpatrick & Hopkins, 1981, 1988; Hopkins, 1989), I have already mentioned that no fewer than 60% of those seen were, at the time of the consultation, anxious about the possibility of organic illness. We found that, three weeks after the consultation, 60% of this group were completely reassured, and a further 28% partly reassured. One year after the consultation, 71% of all patients felt that their headaches were less frequent, and 59% that their headaches were less severe in terms of the pain experienced before consultation. Table 5.4 shows a significant relationship between the outcome at one year, at least in regard to severity of headache, and whether or not the patient had been satisfied with his neurological consultation nearly one year before. Table 5.4 alone shows that, regardless of any technical intervention, satisfaction with the consultation has an important bearing upon outcome. Another outcome measure that Fitzpatrick and I used was the consultation rate for headaches following the neurological consultation (Fig. 5.2). It can be seen that for the vast majority of patients, consultation rates with GPs decreased substantially in the year following the out-patient visit. Of the 74 patients studied, the GP consultation rate decreased for 57, stayed the same for 12 and increased for only five.

From my study with Fitzpatrick, the following general observations can be made about our sample of patients with chronic headache not due to obvious structural disease. The great majority are psychiatrically normal. Real fears about the possibility of organic illness, most usually about the possibility of a brain tumour or impending stroke, are shown by 60%. It was usually comparatively easy to allay these fears, and such reassurance was not related to the extent of investigation. Nonetheless, about one-third of all patients were dissatisfied with their neurological consultation, most commonly with the superficial and routine way in which the neurologist

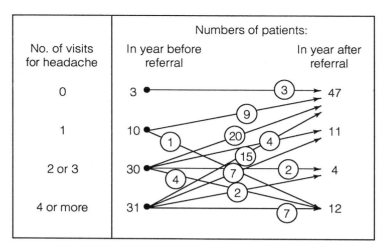

Fig. 5.2. Effect of neurological consultation on general practitioner consultations for headache (from Fitzpatrick & Hopkins, 1981; reproduced by permission of the Journal of Neurology, Neurosurgery and Psychiatry)

went through their story, and because of an inadequate discussion of what headaches meant to the patient in terms of everyday life, the cause of their headaches, and how they could be avoided in the future. Whether or not the patient was satisfied soon after the consultation proved to be a variable in determining the outcome with regard to severity of headache one year later. A consultation by a neurologist does, for many patients, effectively relieve the burden of general practitioner consultations about headache for at least one year. For those patients who cannot be reassured, and who firmly demand further opinions and investigation, specialist help is required.

We should also explore ways of helping patients with chronic symptoms not due to obvious structural disease by methods which do not involve medical skills and consumption of resources. An innovative study by Winkler *et al* (1989) has demonstrated the clinical effectiveness of adding a behavioural self-management programme to the existing management of chronic headache. The frequency, intensity, and duration of headache episodes were reduced significantly more by the self-care behavioural programme than by the standard control management programme. Treatment gains by self care did not deteriorate with time but tended, if anything, to increase over a follow-up period of 12 months. Moreover, those in the self-care group felt more confident in their ability to control headaches through their own efforts without the aid of drugs. Their doctors also thought that they were better. Unfortunately, Winkler's study showed that there was no evidence that the self-care programme reduced costs or the utilisation of health services.

Kroenke (1986) thoughtfully reviews some of the general problems of out-patient clinics:

"Obstacles are omnipresent. Time is short. Problem lists are long. Chief complaints are often nebulous, vexatious or mundane. The scholarly work-up of complex cases is eclipsed by elementary complaints demanding efficient dispensation. The glories of in-patient training give way to the simpler necessities of office practice."

Kroenke goes on to list principles that might improve our ability to cope well with the management of chronic illness in out-patients, whether due to significant organic illness or not. With reference to patients with headaches, I find Kroenke's following observations particularly useful – that current symptoms are of greatest interest to the patient; that it is best to cover one aspect well, rather than many indifferently; that both doctor and patient must be prepared to tolerate some uncertainty; that it is often enough to identify what a symptom is not; and that it is necessary to understand and work within the constraints of each patient's therapeutic personality.

References

DRUMMOND, P. O. & LANCE, J. W. (1984) Clinical diagnosis and computer analysis of headache symptoms. *Journal of Neurology, Neurosurgery and Psychiatry*, **47**, 128–133.

FITZPATRICK, R. M. & HOPKINS, A. (1981) Referrals to neurologists for headaches not due to structural disease. *Journal of Neurology, Neurosurgery and Psychiatry*, **44**, 1061–1067.

—— & —— (1988) Illness behaviour and headache, and the sociology of consultations for headache. In *Headache: Problems in Diagnosis and Management* (ed. A. Hopkins), pp. 349–385. London: Saunders.

GARVEY, M. J. (1985) Occurrence of headaches in anxiety disordered patients. *Headache*, **25**, 101–103.

——, SCHAFFER, C. B. & TUASON, V. B. (1983) Relationship of headache to depression. *British Journal of Psychiatry*, **143**, 544–547.

HENRYK-GUTT, R. & REES, W. L. (1973) Psychological aspects of migraine. *Journal of Psychosomatic Research*, **17**, 141–153.

HOLM, J. E., HOLROYD, K. A., HURSEY, K. G., *et al* (1986) The role of stress in recurrent tension headache. *Headache*, **26**, 160–167.

HOPKINS, A. (1988) A neurologist's approach to patients with headache. In *Headache: Problems in Diagnosis and Management* (ed. A. Hopkins), pp. 37–76. London: Saunders.

—— (1989) Clinical features and appropriate investigations in neurological practice. In *Appropriate Investigation and Treatment in Clinical Practice* (ed. A. Hopkins). London: The Royal College of Physicians.

——, MENKEN, M. & DeFRIESE, G. (1989*a*) A record of patient encounters in neurological practice in the United Kingdom. *Journal of Neurology, Neurosurgery and Psychiatry*, **52**, 436–438.

——, ——, ——, *et al* (1989*b*) Differences in strategies for the diagnosis and treatment of neurological disease among British and American neurologists. *Archives of Neurology*, **46**, 1142–1149.

INTERNATIONAL HEADACHE SOCIETY (1988) Classification and diagnostic criteria for headache disorders, cranial neuralgias and facial pain. *Cephalalgia*, **8** (suppl. 7), 1–96.

KROENKE, K. (1986) Ambulatory care: practice imperfect. *American Journal of Medicine*, **80**, 339–342.

LARSON, E. B., OMENN, G. S. & LEWIS, H. (1980) Diagnostic evaluation of headache. Impact of computerised tomography and cost effectiveness. *Journal of the American Medical Association*, **243**, 359–362.

LAURITZEN, M., SKYHOJ OLSEN, T., LASSEN, N. A., *et al* (1983) The changes of regional cerebral blood flow during the course of classical migraine attacks. *Annals of Neurology*, **13**, 633–641.

LINET, M. S., STEWART, W. F., CELENTANO, D. D., *et al* (1989) An epidemiologic study of headache among adolescents and young adults. *Journal of the American Medical Association*, **261**, 2211–2216.

MUNSAT, T. L., SKERRY, L., KORF, B., *et al* (1990) Phenotypic heterogeneity of spinal muscular atrophy mapping to chromosome 5q 11.2–13.3 (SMA 5q). *Neurology*, **40**, 1831–1836.

NEWLAND, C. A., ILLIS, L. S., ROBINSON, P. K., *et al* (1978) A survey of headache in an English city. *Research and Clinical Studies in Headache*, **5**, 1–20.

NEWMAN, G. (1931) Preventive medicine for the medical student. *Lancet*, *ii*, 1113–1116.

OFFICE OF POPULATION CENSUSES AND SURVEYS (1974) *Second National Morbidity Study*. London: HMSO.

—— (1986) *Morbidity Statistics from General Practice. Third National Study*. London: HMSO.

PACKARD, R. C. (1979) What does the headache patient want? *Headache*, **19**, 370–374.

PIKOFF, H. (1984) Is the muscular model of headache still viable? *Headache*, **24**, 186–198.

PHILIPS, H. C. & HUNTER, M. S. (1982) A psychophysiological investigation of tension headache. *Headache*, **22**, 173–179.

WATERS, W. E. (1986) *Headache*. Beckenham: Croom Helm.

WING, J. K., COOPER, J. E. & SARTORIUS, N. (1974) *Description and Classification of Psychiatric Symptoms*. London: Cambridge University Press.

WINKLER, R., UNDERWOOD, P., FATOVICH, B., *et al* (1989) A clinical trial of a self-care approach to the clinical management of chronic headache in general practice. *Social Science and Medicine*, **29**, 213–219.

ZIEGLER, D. K., HASSANEIN, R. S. & COUCH, J. R. (1982) Headache syndromes suggested by statistical analysis of headache symptoms. *Cephalalgia*, **2**, 125–134.

6 A model of non-organic disorders

FRANCIS CREED

Patients with non-organic disorders tend to be repeatedly investigated in a variety of out-patient clinics for several reasons (Kroenke & Mangelsdorff, 1989). Firstly, doubts may linger in the doctor's mind that organic disease has remained undetected in previous investigations. Secondly, the patient and/or the relatives may demand further tests. Thirdly, the doctor is not sufficiently confident in making an alternative (non-organic) diagnosis. By summarising the preceding chapters it is hoped that a model of these complaints can be developed which will help the physician understand, and manage rationally, these disorders.

The first step in understanding these symptoms is to compare those presenting in the clinic with similar symptoms reported by non-consulters in the community. Evidence has been presented in Chapter 1 that the symptoms presenting in the clinic, at least in the example of abdominal pain, are more severe than those experienced by non-consulters. These patients are presumably predisposed to develop more severe abdominal symptoms when under stress.

Nearly half of the clinic patients reported in Chapter 1 also had marked symptoms of anxiety and depression, in line with several other studies (Chapter 2). Evidence was presented in Chapter 2 of the role played by psychiatric disorders in causing or exacerbating the symptoms. Such anxiety or depression may also play a part in explaining why the patient seeks medical attention at that particular time (Colgan *et al*, 1988). However, diagnosable psychiatric disorder is only found in a small proportion of these patients (it was as low as 16% in the headache patients) so there must be a more widespread explanation for seeking medical advice. This is likely to be an underlying fear of severe illness, which was found in 60% of headache patients and 80% of consulters with dyspepsia, compared with 20% of dyspeptic non-consulters in the community (Lydeard & Jones, 1989).

Fears of illness and medical reassurance

In Chapter 5, Dr Hopkins shows how patients are generally reassured by a clear explanation for their headache, whether or not investigations had been performed. Such patients may then cease further medical consultations. However, a minority will continue to pursue neurological investigations, indicating a belief that underlying organic disease has been missed. Another group of patients may be reassured that there is no intracerebral disease, and cease neurological consultations, yet continue to consult their general practitioner (GP) frequently with other complaints (Grove *et al*, 1980), indicating an underlying psychological or social problem that generates concern about possible serious illness.

Thus the following factors have been implicated in explaining why these disorders are presenting in the clinic:

(a) the somatic symptoms (e.g. abdominal pain or headache) are severe
(b) there is a clear psychiatric disorder in a minority of patients
(c) the patients have fears of serious illness
(d) there is an underlying psychological or social problem.

The next step is to understand why and how these somatic symptoms come about. The following case report demonstrates how fears of illness arose in one patient.

Case report

A 62-year-old manager lost his voice through laryngitis. He became concerned that he might have throat cancer following a chance remark about an acquaintance whose cancer had presented with loss of voice. For this reason he sought medical reassurance, and underwent a complete check up during which mildly abnormal liver function tests (Gilbert's syndrome) were discovered. This led to an escalation of his worries and he repeatedly visited the physician seeking reassurance. His concerns became understandable only when it transpired that he had lost three brothers. Two had died in their thirties, one with a stroke and the other with ischaemic heart disease. The third had died recently. After each of the two earlier deaths he had experienced a period of increased anxiety about his health. After the first death he feared that a 'normal' headache indicated an imminent stroke. After the second brother died, he became preoccupied about every minor discomfort in his chest. The current symptoms had no such direct link to his most recent brother's death, but were linked to a concern about his son's mild illness, which might upset his forthcoming wedding. On physical examination there were no abnormalities, but throughout the patient quizzed the doctor as to the nature of his abdominal pains (which were trivial) and whether they signified serious liver disease.

In this patient, there were two immediate precipitants of the illness concern: minor physical pathology (laryngitis) and the current psychological concern of the forthcoming wedding (the first brother had died shortly after his marriage). There was also the more distant predisposing factor: the previous sensitising effect of the three brothers' deaths.

This example also illustrates how fears of organic disease can lead to medical referral even in the absence of formal psychiatric disorder; there was no frank anxiety state yet the patient was greatly concerned that he might have physical disease, as witnessed by his excessive requests for reassurance during the physical examination. It is helpful for both doctor and patient to note that there were previous episodes of excessive illness concern in the past, which, like the present episode, become fully understandable, provided the appropriate information is elicited.

The additional information about the man's life situation at the time of presentation is crucial to understanding the problem. Without such information the clinical problem may be regarded as a slightly annoying patient who refuses to be reassured despite the doctor's best efforts. Thus the doctor must decide which is more useful in a particular case – performing investigations for possible organic disease, in the hopes of reassuring the patient (Sox *et al*, 1981), or gathering additional information with which to explain why the patient experiences the symptoms and concomitant distress. Often it is the latter which is most helpful to the patient (Thomas, 1987).

Attribution

A key feature of this type of clinical presentation is the belief that the symptoms are due to physical illness. The frightening nature of the chest pain, or the persistent nature of abdominal pain, may in itself cause anxiety. The ensuing investigations, if their purpose is not properly explained, may do nothing to allay that fear. They may even be misinterpreted by the anxious patient as an indication that the doctor believes organic disease is a distinct possibility. The bald statement that 'nothing is wrong' is clearly untrue and does little to reassure many patients.

The tendency to attribute minor physical ailments, or even normal physiological sensations, to serious disease, is something that may be reinforced by other family members or friends. This can contribute to the patient's anxiety by likening the patient's chest pain to that of a relative who died of a myocardial infarction, or by refusing to allow the patient to return to normal activities. One aspect of the doctor's task is therefore to help the patient reattribute the symptoms to a psychological rather than a physical basis (see Chapter 7). This may involve a discussion with the patient and his or her relative if the latter is to stop encouraging the patient that further investigations should be sought.

These various factors which help us to understand why fears of illness arise are those summarised in Fig. 4.1 (p. 27). The next section provides a basis for assessment in the clinic.

Characteristics of the presenting symptoms

The following aspects of history-taking may enable the physician to decide that the presenting symptom is much more likely to be explained on the basis of a psychological problem than on that of organic disease (Cohen, 1982).

(a) *Additional somatic symptoms*. The patient who presents with chest pain may present a difficult diagnostic problem, especially if the pain is severe and its description sounds suspiciously like that of angina. Closer questioning may reveal, however, that numerous other somatic symptoms outside the cardiovascular system, accompany the chest pain. These may include abdominal churning ('butterflies'), a sensation of light-headedness, an urge to micturate or 'diarrhoea', wobbly legs, difficulty breathing, a tightness in the throat and paraesthesia, any or all of which may have accompanied the chest pain. Palpitations are particularly common. There is often a feeling of panic and the patient reports: "I thought I was having a heart attack [or stroke]".

(b) *Precipitation by a psychological factor*. It usually becomes clear that the chest pain is not precipitated by exercise (occasionally it is). Common precipitants are:

(i) the mention of heart disease in conversation, the newspaper, or on television, which reminds the patient of his/her fears

(ii) a particular situation commonly associated with anxiety, e.g. shops, crowd, lifts

(iii) a personally difficult situation, e.g. an argument, reminders of relationship problems or other failures.

In addition the person might be remarkably symptom-free when away from the precipitant, e.g. while on holiday.

(c) *Associated symptoms of psychiatric disorder*. In some of the patients with these disorders there is an overt anxiety or depressive disorder. The doctor should therefore systematically inquire about feelings of tension, worry and depression. Impairments of sleep, appetite, concentration, and libido should be specifically sought. These psychiatric symptoms will frequently have commenced at the time of the somatic symptoms, often in response to a clear life event. The presence of psychiatric disorder may lead to the problem becoming severe and disabling as in the following example.

Case report

A 40-year-old lorry driver was admitted as an urgent case with chest pain possibly due to cardiac ischaemia, for which there was no positive evidence. It turned out that this had occurred on and off for three years and had been investigated at three previous hospitals. On each occasion the patient had understood the doctors to say "there is nothing wrong with you", which eventually led him to wonder if he was a hypochondriac. His own GP had reassured him that this was not the case by stating: "something *is* wrong but I don't know what". Only one doctor had decreased the patient's fears about serious physical disease, but this had been temporary.

On two occasions he had a positive diagnosis from the doctor. After gastroscopy at one previous admission he had been told that his symptoms were due to oesophagitis, but the resulting medication had not helped the chest pain so his continuing symptoms were a continued cause for concern. The next doctor was a gastroenterologist who made a positive diagnosis of irritable bowel syndrome. The patient was impressed by this doctor because he had asked him about gut, chest and neurological symptoms, all of which the patient had experienced. The patient had left the consultation "with a load lifted from my mind". He continued to feel better until another doctor disputed the diagnosis! This illustrates the power of a positive diagnosis (Sox *et al*, 1981) but also the dangers of conflicting advice.

When referred to a psychiatrist the following history emerged:

(a) The symptoms occurred in a crowd, following a disagreement or if he sat and thought about illness
(b) The original episode of chest pain had occurred at the time he discovered that his wife's breast lump was malignant
(c) The second major episode had occurred at the time his twin brother had a myocardial infarct
(d) At interview, discussion of his life situation (he had lost his job as a driver because of dizziness and his marriage appeared to be under great strain) brought on sweating, stomach churning and chest discomfort.

Thus, the main features of the aetiology of this man's chest pain were as follows. He was predisposed to develop chest pain because of his habits: heavy smoking and drinking are known to be associated with chest pain. The stresses associated with onset were his wife's breast cancer and his brother's myocardial infarct. There were clear symptoms of an anxiety state. The illness was maintained by the continuing psychosocial problems of losing his job (and consequent time to brood on his illness) and the deteriorating marital relationship. His worries were perpetuated by the continuing symptoms and the lack of a satisfactory explanation or effective treatment.

Once all these pieces of jigsaw were put together both doctor and patient felt quite confident that anxiety and illness fears could explain the chest pain. The doctor explained the vicious cycle of anxiety–palpitations–chest pain– increased anxiety (Chapter 9) and the patient was much relieved. He was offered psychological treatment for his anxiety and recovered completely.

From the evidence cited earlier in this book and illustrations in this chapter, a model of non-organic disorders can be proposed:

(a) Predisposition: autonomic sensitivity, previous illness experience
(b) Factors associated with onset: severe life event, minor physical pathology
(c) Associated symptoms: other somatic symptoms, psychiatric disorder?
(d) Exacerbating factors (triggered by certain situations, rather than 'physical' factors)
(e) Maintaining factors: environmental stress, no understanding of symptoms, illness fears reinforced by relative?

In complex cases all, or most, of these aspects of the model may be identified. In more straightforward cases one or two aspects only will be present. Doctors who use this model will be more confident in explaining to patients the origin of their somatic symptoms.

References

COHEN, S. I. (1982) The evaluation of patients with somatic symptoms – the "difficult" diagnostic problem. In *Medicine and Psychiatry – A Practical Approach* (eds F. H. Creed & J. M. Pfeffer). London: Pitman.

COLGAN, S., CREED, F. H. & KLASS, H. (1988) Symptom complaints, psychiatric disorder and abnormal illness behaviour in patients with upper abdominal pain. *Psychological Medicine*, **18**, 887–892.

GROVE, J. L., BUTLER, P. & MILLAC, P. A. H. (1980) The effect of a visit to a neurological clinic upon patients with tension headache. *The Practitioner*, **224**, 195–196.

KROENKE, K. & MANGELSDORFF, D. (1989) Common symptoms in ambulatory care: incidence, evaluation, therapy and outcome. *American Journal of Medicine*, **86**, 262–266.

LYDEARD, S. & JONES, R. (1989) Factors affecting the decision to consult with dyspepsia: comparison of consulters and non-consulters. *Journal of the Royal College of General Practitioners*, **39**, 495–498.

SOX, H. C. Jr, MARGULIES, I. & SOX, C. H. (1981) Psychologically mediated effects of diagnostic tests. *Annals of International Medicine*, **95**, 680–685.

THOMAS, K. B. (1987) General practice consultations: is there any point in being positive? *British Medical Journal*, **294**, 1200–1202.

7 The management of medical out-patients with non-organic disorders: the reattribution model

DAVID GOLDBERG

Most patients seen in general practice settings with diagnosable psychiatric disorders are not seeking help for psychological complaints, but for physical symptoms. These physical symptoms may accompany true physical illnesses, but often cannot be attributed entirely to these illnesses; or they may occur in the absence of any diagnosable physical illness.

In a large multi-practice study of patients coming to general practice clinics with new episodes of illness, the figures shown in Table 7.1 were obtained (Goldberg & Bridges, 1988). We considered that the patient was 'somatising' if four criteria were met:

(a) the patient was seeking help for physical complaints
(b) the patient did not attribute these complaints to a psychological cause
(c) a psychiatric disorder could be diagnosed according to objective research criteria
(d) the presenting complaints were either exacerbated or caused by the psychiatric disorder.

If there was any doubt about the final point, the case was assessed as being one of 'unrelated' physical and psychological ill-health.

It can be seen that no fewer than 19% of all new illnesses fulfilled these criteria, and that these illnesses were in fact the most frequent way in which psychiatric disorder manifested itself in general medical settings. It is noteworthy that in the presence of a real physical disease, only one-third of these psychological disorders was detected by the general practitioner (GP) seeing the patient. It can be seen that 'somatising' patients without physical illness are highly likely to have their psychological distress detected by their doctor. However, the presence of a real physical illness serves to distract the doctor from the psychological distress.

It is not known what the distribution of such cases would be in the medical out-patients department of the general hospital, although it is known that psychiatric disorders are equally common in these clinical settings (for

TABLE 7.1

Research diagnoses made by a research psychiatrist's ratings combined with assessments of physical illness by family doctors for 590 new illnesses (from Goldberg & Bridges, 1988)

Category	All patients (n = 590)	Probability of detection by family doctor
Physical illnesses without psychiatric disorder	67%	NA
Physical illness and unrelated psychiatric disorder	8%	19%
Physical illness with secondary psychiatric disorder	1%	74%
Somatisation	19%	47%
physical illness with symptoms exacerbated or caused by psychiatric disorder	13.5%	33%
somatised psychiatric illnesses (no diagnosable physical illness)	5.5%	85%
Psychiatric disorders presenting with psychological symptoms	5%	95%

reviews, see Goldberg, 1989; Burvill, 1990; Lobo, 1990). In the presence of a coexisting physical disease, doctors either extend their concept of what symptoms can be produced by that disease, or rate the patient as having 'functional overlay'.

A model for intervention

In view of the ubiquity of somatisation, we sought a model for managing such cases which could be taught to trainee GPs. We based this on what experienced psychiatrists and doctors with an interest in psychosomatic medicine tend to do with such patients. The essence of the intervention is to help patients change their attribution of the cause of their symptoms from a physical explanation to one which allows them to appreciate the possible importance of psychological factors. If this can be achieved, the patient is more likely to cooperate with attempts to help them by discussing social and interpersonal problems, or by prescribing antidepressant medication.

Our model for training GPs emerged from my own experience in having watched over 1000 videotapes of actual encounters between GPs and their patients, from the clinical experience of what seemed to work with the patients referred to us from general practice, and perhaps most of all from discussions with Dr A. T. Lesser of McMaster University, whose 'problem-based interviewing' (Lesser, 1985) forms part of our basic training package for improving the psychological skills of trainee family doctors. The training package that emerged was then discussed further with experienced family doctors, and modified in the light of these discussions.

Three stages in the clinical encounter

(a) *Feeling understood*. It is impossible to change a patient's attribution of the cause of symptoms until the doctor has completed the history and physical examination, and has received the results of any investigations that are deemed necessary. However, much needs to be done before this point if reattribution is to be successful. The first stage of the interview then is that which leads up to the point at which the doctor is in a position to begin the process of reattribution. We believe that the doctor is much more likely to succeed if the patient feels that his/her problems have been understood.

There is nothing particularly recondite about the processes that cause patients to feel that their problems have been understood, and most experienced and sensitive doctors routinely carry out most or all of the processes that we have identified at this stage. However, it has been our experience that doctors who regularly experience difficulties in getting patients to alter their attributions often do not carry out these procedures well. They do not:

(a) take a full history of the pain, elicit other associated symptoms, ask about a typical pain day
(b) respond to mood 'cues': clarify complaints, make empathic comments, probe mood state with directive questions
(c) explore family and social factors
(d) explore patient's health beliefs
(e) carry out necessary physical examination (investigations only if indicated).

(b) *Changing the agenda*. It is not enough to tell a patient that one has examined him and found no cause for his pain, since this often makes patients think that they are thought to be imagining their pains. If the doctor goes on to say that the pain is of nervous origin, and suggests a psychotropic, the patient is convinced that this is what the doctor thinks, and patient and doctor begin to drift apart. The important thing to do is to summarise the physical findings and then to acknowledge the reality of the pain in a sympathetic way, for example:

> "You are rather tender over your large gut, but apart from that I have not found anything abnormal in your tummy. But you have been getting a lot of discomfort, haven't you?"

The doctor then goes on to re-frame the complaints by summarising other symptoms and mentioning life events:

> "People can get bad pains like this when they are upset, and I'm struck by the fact that since your mother died you mentioned that you have been crying a lot and waking up early . . . ."

In summary, this vital stage consists of three simple steps, none of which can be omitted:

(a) Feed back results of the physical examination
(b) Acknowledge the reality of the pain
(c) Re-frame the patient's complaint, mentioning other symptoms and any life events

If this stage is handled well, the final stage can then be introduced.

(c) *Making the link.* The aim of the final stage is to provide the patient with an explanation of how the psychological stress or disorder that you have identified may be actually producing the symptoms, and to do this in a way that is appropriate to the particular symptom, and which is understandable to the patient. There is of course no single explanation that fills the bill, and the doctor's task is to choose an appropriate explanation for the patient being seen. The six possible explanations that we teach in our learning package are as follows:

(a) Simple explanation: how anxiety causes somatic symptoms
(b) Simple explanation: how depression causes somatic symptoms
(c) Demonstration: practical (for example, holding a book in an outstretched hand demonstrates how pain results from tense muscles)
(d) Demonstration: life events (for example, how pain is worse on days faced with relevant stress)
(e) Demonstration: here and now, as we talk about it (relevant stress, e.g. I notice you hold your tummy)
(f) Projection: other family members may have had similar somatic symptoms when under stress

Explanations given to patients should ideally be in two stages: how stress alters a physiological mechanism, which in turn causes a pain. For example "when people are very anxious the muscles in the wall of their gut can go into spasm, and this causes pain in your tummy and is the reason that your gut felt tender when I examined it"; or "when people are depressed it alters their pain threshold so that a pain that could be tolerated when they are well is felt as being very much worse than it otherwise would".

Designing the original package

Our previous experience in teaching medical interview techniques to medical students and GPs had led us to believe that feedback of actual interview performance is a powerful method of changing a doctor's interview style (Maguire *et al*, 1976; Goldberg *et al*, 1980). However, before this is done, it is advantageous to split a complex skill down into its component parts and to practise each one separately, a process called teaching microskills

(Ivey, 1971). We had previously designed a package to teach psychotherapeutic skills to psychiatrists in training. The package consists of an introductory videotape demonstrating the component parts of a psychotherapist's skills, followed by a tape which allows students to practise each skill separately (Maguire *et al*, 1984).

We adapted this technique for the present purpose, making instructional videotapes which were shown to 22 general practice trainees on the first day of their training course with us (Goldberg *et al*, 1989). After an introductory lecture, trainees viewed the demonstration videotape and discussed it. After lunch, they divided into pairs to watch the micro-teaching videotape which provided opportunities for them to practise each skill separately. Within each pair, trainees took turns in role-playing the doctor and the patient, and the videotape provided details of each clinical enactment. Teachers moved round the room in which this occurred, providing comments to the trainees on their performance. Trainees had opportunities to receive video-feedback teaching about their interviews with patients in the weeks after they had been exposed to the learning package.

The trainees had each interviewed a role-played patient before the course began, and they repeated this at the end of the course. Videotapes of these encounters were rated by observers blind to whether the recording was made before or after training. There were significant improvements in four of the eight skills tested in part (a) ('feeling understood'), in three of the four skills in part (b) ('changing the agenda'), and there was a significant increase in use of any part (c) strategy ('making the link') (Gask *et al*, 1989).

Amendments to the training package

We used our experience with this evaluation to improve our videotaped learning package: improvements included replacement of about 50% of the case examples with better enactments, and sharpening up our explanations for several of the 'making the link' strategies. The new learning package showed better results with our course in 1990, although the improvements were not dramatic – ten of the skills were now improved, compared with only eight with the earlier package. However, it should be emphasised that the method of assessment, depending as it does on a single role-played interview, would be most unlikely to produce significant improvements in all areas. It would be quite inappropriate to offer a single patient five different explanations for their symptoms, and indeed it would not be possible to do this in the time available for the interview.

It is also noteworthy that the reason that two of the 'changing the agenda' skills were no longer significant in 1989 was that this group of trainees were actually good at these two skills before the course, so that a significant improvement was more difficult to achieve (Table 7.2).

TABLE 7.2

Results of training courses in two consecutive years; for 20 GP trainees (1988 course – Gask et al, 1989) and 18 GP trainees (1989 course – Kaaya et al, 1990)

	1988 course: improvement	*1989 course: improvement*
Feeling understood		
Taking a full history of pain		
asks about radiation	NS	$P<0.05$
typical pain day	NS	$P<0.05$
elicits associated symptoms	$P<0.05$	NS
Cue source		
delayed verbal	NS	NS
non-verbal	$P<0.05$	NS
Empathic statements	$P<0.05$	$P<0.05$
Explore social and family factors	$P<0.05$	$P<0.05$
Explore health beliefs	NS	$P<0.05$
Changing the agenda		
Feed back results of examination	NS	$P<0.05$
Acknowledge reality of symptoms	$P<0.05$	$P<0.05$
Summarise mood symptoms	$P<0.05$	NS
Summarise life events	$P<0.05$	NS
Making the link		
Any strategy	$P<0.05$	$P<0.05$
Explanation (depression or anxiety)	NS	$P<0.05$
Practical demonstration	NS	$P<0.05$
Life event demonstration	NS	NS
Here and now demonstration	NS	NS
Projection – family member	NS	NS

Adapting the training for doctors

If these strategies can be shown to be successful in improving the outcome of somatised distress syndromes, they will have to be incorporated into routine training programmes administered by general practitioner teachers. However, it is important to stress that this package has not yet received this essential piece of validation. If it ever does, it will be necessary to ask how hospital-based doctors, who do not have the same tradition of using videotapes to improve their interview performance, can be expected to benefit from such a training package.

We have shown that the most effective learning experience for psychiatrists who are to teach interviewing techniques to medical students, and for GPs providing interview training, is that they should themselves undergo the training experience they will be giving to their students (Naji *et al*, 1986; Gask *et al*, 1991). Such training experiences are quite brief. Teaching from one's own professional group is probably more appropriate than supposing that psychiatrists should be responsible for all such teaching. The role of psychiatrists is to produce and evaluate the training packages, and to assist their senior colleagues in other disciplines in providing this kind of training to their juniors.

Conclusion

Psychologically distressed people often present somatic symptoms to doctors, and the psychological distress is especially likely to be overlooked if the patient happens to have a coexistent physical illness. Such patients are often referred to hospital clinics for further evaluation. It is not enough for doctors to see their role entirely in terms of the exclusion of physical causes for the presenting symptoms. We should be able to do better than that. A training package has been described which is intended to speed up the process of learning to help patients to attribute their symptoms to psychological and social causes. Such packages will probably not be effective unless doctors in training are prepared to record their interviews with patients, and submit these to peer review. The training package merely provides a framework for such training, and perhaps helps to speed up the process of acquisition of new clinical skills.

References

BURVILL, P. (1990) The epidemiology of psychological disorders in general medical settings. In *Psychological Disorders in General Medical Settings* (eds N. Sartorius, D. Goldberg & G. de Girolamo, *et al*) pp. 9–20. Bern: Hofgrefe-Huber.

GASK, L., GOLDBERG, D., PORTER, R., *et al* (1989) The treatment of somatisation: evaluation of a teaching package with general practice trainees. *Journal of Psychosomatic Research, 33*, 697–703.

——, ——, BOARDMAN, J., *et al* (1991) Training general practitioners to teach psychiatric interviewing skills. *Medical Education* (in press).

GOLDBERG, D. (1989) Mental health aspects of general health care. In *Health and Behaviour* (eds D. Hamburg, & N. Sartorius), pp. 162–177. Cambridge: Cambridge University Press.

——, STEELE, J., SMITH, C., *et al* (1980) Training family doctors to recognise psychiatric illness with increased accuracy. *Lancet, ii*, 521–523.

—— & BRIDGES, K. (1988) Somatic presentations of psychiatric illness in primary care settings. *Journal of Psychosomatic Research, 32*, 137–144.

——, GASK, L., & O'DOWD, T. (1989) The treatment of somatisation: teaching techniques of reattribution. *Journal of Psychosomatic Research, 33*, 689–695.

IVEY, A. (1971) *Microcounselling: Innovations in Interview Training*. Springfield, Illinois: Thomas.

KAAYA, S., GOLDBERG, D. & GASK, L. (1991) The management of somatic presentations of psychiatric illness in general medical settings: evaluation of a new training course for general practitioners. *Medical Education* (in press).

LESSER, A. T. (1985) Problem-based interviewing in general practice: a model. *Medical Education, 19*, 299–304.

LOBO, A. (1990) Mental health in general medical clinics. In *The Public Health Impact of Mental Disorder* (eds D. Goldberg & D. Tantam), pp. 45–53. Bern: Hogrefe-Huber.

MAGUIRE, P., ROE, P., GOLDBERG, D., *et al* (1978) The value of feedback in teaching interviewing skills to medical students. *Psychological Medicine, 8*, 695–704.

——, GOLDBERG, D., HOBSON, R., *et al* (1984) Evaluating the teaching of a method of psychotherapy. *British Journal of Psychiatry, 144*, 575–580.

NAJI, S., MAGUIRE, G., FAIRBURN, S., *et al* (1986) Training clinical teachers to teach interviewing skills to medical students. *Medical Education, 20*, 140–147.

8 The management of medical out-patients with non-organic disorders: the irritable bowel syndrome

ELSPETH GUTHRIE

This chapter has three main sections. The first outlines a randomised controlled trial of psychotherapy in patients with refractory irritable bowel syndrome (IBS). The second section describes the nature of the psychological treatment approach employed in the trial, and the final section discusses the similarities and differences between the various psychological approaches that have been used in out-patients with refractory IBS.

A clinical trial

Harvey *et al* (1987) demonstrated that the majority of out-patients with IBS (up to 83%) respond to conventional medical treatment in conjunction with explanation and reassurance, and it is doubtful whether a psychological approach is warranted or justified in these cases. A small group of patients, however, remain unresponsive to treatment and tend to run a chronic course, undergoing many investigations and utilising a great deal of health service resources (Kingham & Dawson, 1985). Our Manchester treatment trial was only concerned with this type of patient. They should not be regarded as being representative of most out-patients with IBS.

The trial was a randomised, controlled trial of brief, dynamic psychotherapy versus supportive listening, in out-patients with refractory IBS (Fig. 8.1). Patients were maintained on their medical treatment, which was unchanged during the 12-week trial. All patients received a long initial assessment session. The treatment group then received six sessions of psychotherapy; the control group received five sessions of supportive listening. Supportive listening was used to control for the non-specific effects of psychological intervention, in other words the so-called placebo effect of seeing a kind and supportive doctor who listens.

Patients were comprehensively assessed at the beginning and end of the trial period. They completed self-rating scales for physical and psychological

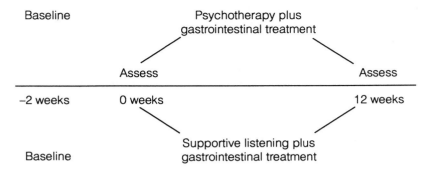

Fig. 8.1. Design of the trial

symptoms. Their bowel symptoms were rated independently by a gastroenterologist who remained blind to the trial groups. In addition, patients were asked to complete a daily diary bowel chart of their gastrointestinal function for the duration of the trial.

Consecutive patients fulfilling the following criteria were approached to participate in the trial.

(a) Irritable bowel syndrome – i.e. abdominal pain, abdominal distension and abnormal bowel habit associated with normal haematology, rectal biopsy, colonoscopy etc.
(b) Continuous symptoms for at least one year
(c) Attendance at gastrointestinal clinic for at least six months
(d) Unresponsive to conventional medical treatment
(e) No age limit
(f) Patients not excluded if receiving invalidity benefit or marked evidence of psychiatric illness.

The gastroenterologist briefly described the trial to the patient, and then the psychiatrist, who was present in the clinic, took the patient to another room to explain the trial in more detail. This meant that the patient was able to meet the psychiatrist from the outset, and many of the patient's fears regarding the involvement of a psychiatrist could be allayed at this point. Following recruitment, patients were randomly allocated to either the treatment or the control group.

There were 115 patients who fulfilled the trial criteria. Five patients were excluded because of severe suicidal ideation. Only four patients refused to take part. Two patients could not speak English and two patients were later withdrawn because underlying organic pathology was discovered; one of these was found to have chronic pancreatitis and the other had inflammatory bowel disease. Therefore, 53 patients were allocated to the treatment group and 49 to the control group. The results are reported in detail elsewhere (Guthrie *et al*, 1991) and so are only be briefly described in this chapter.

There was no difference in the psychological and physical ratings of symptoms between the treatment and control groups at the beginning of the study. At the end of the trial, however, the treatment group showed a significant improvement in both physical and psychological symptoms in comparison with the control group. Fig. 8.2 depicts the daily ratings of abdominal pain by the patients throughout the trial period. Fig. 8.3 shows a variety of ratings of the patients' gastrointestinal symptoms for the treatment and control group, at the beginning and end of the trial. Fig. 8.3(b) shows the gastroenterologist's independent ratings. There was a trend for both men and women to improve with psychotherapy, but because of the small numbers of men in the treatment group, the improvement did not reach significance for men.

To determine baseline predictors of outcome, the patients who received and completed a full course of psychotherapy were studied separately (Table 8.1). Those with a good outcome, according to the gastroenterologist, were compared with those with a poor outcome. Symptoms of anxiety or depression, and the recognition by patients that stress affected their symptoms, were good predictors of outcome. Poor predictors were the

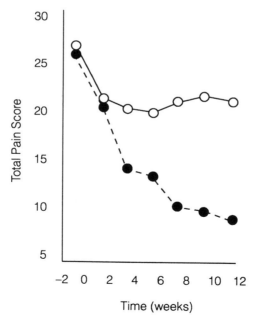

Fig. 8.2. Daily ratings of abdominal pain by treatment group (●---●) and control group (○—○) throughout the 12-week trial (significant difference between groups after week 3)

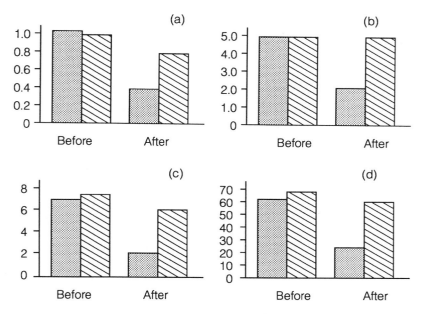

Fig. 8.3. Gastrointestinal symptoms for the treatment (☐) and control (☒) groups. (a) Abdominal symptoms, (b) gastroenterologist ratings, (c) limiting effect of illness and (d) linear analogue scale of symptoms

presence of constant (as opposed to intermittent) abdominal pain and a long duration of the current illness, given that the group as a whole had long-standing symptoms by definition.

Following the end of the trial, patients in the control group, who were still severely distressed by their symptoms, were offered dynamic psychotherapy. These patients also showed a significant improvement in their bowel and psychological symptoms following therapy.

Strenuous efforts were made to follow up all patients who participated in the trial 12 months after completing treatment. Drop-outs were also

TABLE 8.1
Baseline characteristics of improvers v. non-improvers

Characteristics	Improvers (n = 32)	Non-improvers (n = 12)
No. of males	3	2
No. aged over 50 years	15	6
Anxiety/depression	20	3*
Median years current symptoms	2	4.5**
Constant pain	7	8*
Pain worse with stress	20	2*

*$P<0.05$, **$P<0.01$.

reassessed. Most patients who improved with psychotherapy during the trial remained well. Those patients who failed to improve or who dropped out of the study complained of continuing bowel symptoms.

The treatment

Psychodynamic psychotherapy has several important components.

(a) It is a treatment approach through the medium of an intense personal relationship. The degree of intimacy that is established between the doctor and patient means that the patient can begin to discuss and share his/her innermost feelings and fears.

(b) Psychodynamic theory postulates that a significant degree of psychological and physical distress is either caused, or exacerbated, by problems in the patient's life. These problems are usually related to difficulties in the patient's relationships (e.g. the loss of someone close, or the inability to form satisfactory relationships, or unhappiness resulting from dissatisfaction with current relationships).

(c) Because of the intensity of the relationship between doctor and patient, the problems in the patient's life are mirrored or recur in the relationship that the patient forms with the doctor. For example, a patient may have problems in coping with authority figures, and thus develop bowel symptoms before he/she has to present a report to a supervisor. The patient may fear criticism and humiliation by the supervisor, even if in reality he/she is not overtly critical. In psychotherapy, a patient with these kinds of problems will come to perceive the doctor as authoritarian, harsh and critical, even if in reality the doctor is kind and supportive.

(d) These misperceptions of people or distortions in relationships that the patient forms can then be identified.

(e) The link to symptom formation can then be understood.

(f) This leads to a reduction in symptom formation, but also a greater understanding by the patient of the problems in his/her relationships, which can then lead to further change and the development of more mature and realistic relationships. This makes the recurrence of symptoms less likely.

The following case example from the trial illustrates how psychotherapy actually works in practice.

Case report

Bob was a 49-year-old welder, who had suffered from continuous symptoms of abdominal pain and loose motions for four years. His symptoms began following an accident at work involving injuries to his left knee, and he had been unable to work for the last three years.

He was an only child who was brought up by a strict and unaffectionate mother. His father left home when he was six. Bob described himself as a loner with few friends. He found school difficult, was a slow learner, and often played truant. He drank heavily when he was a teenager and received a prison sentence for theft. He married the first woman he met on leaving prison. She was ten years older than him, and taunted and humiliated him in much the same way that his mother had done when he was a child. Following the break-up of his marriage, he lived alone for several years and had no close relationships.

Shortly before his bowel symptoms began, he met an 18-year-old woman with a placid and kind temperament. After a brief courtship, she became pregnant and they subsequently married. Although the symptoms occurred at about the time of their marriage, Bob said that he felt safe with his second wife, that he had never been happier, and could see no connection between his marriage and his bowel symptoms.

Bob was not used to discussing aspects of his life and feelings with others, but he agreed to participate in the trial. As the majority of patients with IBS are not psychologically minded, and strongly believe that their symptoms have an organic aetiology, it is often difficult to engage them in psychotherapy. A powerful way, however, of doing this, is by encouraging patients to describe in detail their physical symptoms. Firstly, this helps to reassure them that the psychiatrist does not think that their symptoms are 'all in the mind'. Secondly, the words that the patient chooses to describe his/her physical symptoms often give the psychiatrist insight into the patient's inner feelings. This is particularly true for bowel symptoms, as many of the words that are used to describe gastrointestinal disturbance are also used to describe emotional states.

Bob described his symptoms.

"It's no good, I can't keep it in, my stomach churns and I just have to go."
"I can't work, I have to keep rushing to the loo."
"It's awful, everything just explodes away from me."
"I just have to go, it's awful, I'm frightened to go out."

I simply fed back his words, removing the references to bowel symptoms.

"Churning inside, can't keep things in."
"Frightened everything will explode."
"Awful . . . frightened."

As the conversation developed, the bowel symptoms were used more and more as a metaphor for the way that Bob felt inside, although no direct links were made between physical symptoms and emotions.

"Can't keep things in."
"When things come out . . . no control."
"A dirty mess inside."
"Full of shit."

Bob gradually began to realise that although I was using virtually the same words that he was using to describe bowel symptoms, I was actually talking about feelings.

After Bob had made this connection, he began to talk more freely about himself. He described in more depth how humiliated he had felt by his first wife, who had particularly belittled his sexual performance, and how dominated he had felt by his mother. I had noticed that Bob had seemed very wary and frightened of me at times in the session, and was also very deferential, and overly polite. After a long pause, I tentatively inquired whether he was worried that I would criticise or humiliate him in some way. At this point, he became deathly white, got up, and rushed out of the room saying that he had to go to the toilet.

After I had shown him to the toilet, he came back with me to the interview room, and sat down in a rather flustered state. We were then able to discuss in much greater depth his fears towards me, how they reminded him of his mother and his first wife, and how they were related to his bowel symptoms, which had just been graphically illustrated in the session. In later sessions, Bob was also able to understand that although he had felt very frightened and intimidated by me, in reality I had not been overtly critical of him, but in fact had been kindly and supportive. He then realised that although his wife in reality was a shy and timid woman (one of the least likely people in the world to criticise him), in the back of his mind he perceived her as frightening and potentially critical, and this had resulted in the development of his bowel symptoms.

His symptoms eased with therapy and he was also able to talk to his wife about his fears of her. This brought them much closer together, and helped to dispel many of his anxieties, thus reducing the likelihood of his symptoms recurring in the future.

This case demonstrates how dynamic psychotherapy can be used to treat patients with non-organic symptoms. Fig. 8.4 summarises the process of therapy. Firstly, the patient has to be engaged by the doctor in the treatment process (not always an easy task). Secondly, the patient is helped to make a link between physical symptoms and feelings; one way of achieving this is through the use of metaphor. Following this, any difficulties or problems in the patient's relationships can be explored.

In Bob's case, an intense relationship between the doctor and patient developed. This resulted in Bob perceiving the doctor as critical and threatening. This distortion or misperception of the doctor was then identified, and linked to early feelings and experiences related to his mother. The link to irrational fears regarding his young wife could then be made and the relationship to the development of his bowel symptoms understood.

Fig. 8.4. *Process of therapy for patients with non-organic symptoms*

Main psychological treatment approaches

Four main psychological approaches have been adopted with patients with refractory IBS. These are: psychodynamic psychotherapy, hypnosis, cognitive–behavioural therapy and psychotropic drugs.

Psychodynamic psychotherapy

This approach has been described in detail above. It involves forming an intense emotional relationship with the patient, linking symptoms to feelings, and then understanding the relationship of symptoms to problems or emotional difficulties in the patient's life. There have been two randomised, controlled trials of this kind of therapy in patients with chronic symptoms of IBS (Svedlund, 1983; Guthrie *et al*, 1991). Both studies recruited patients consecutively and had adequate numbers (102 and 101 patients). Patients do well with psychotherapy if they have overt psychiatric symptoms, and recognise in some way that their symptoms are related to stress. Patients with a long duration of current symptoms (median 4.5 years) and those with atypical symptoms (i.e. constant pain) do less well.

Hypnosis

This approach involves relaxation and suggestion. It is a technique that is taught to the patient to help control and relieve bowel symptoms. It does not involve an intense relationship with the doctor or a discussion of problems or difficulties in the patient's life. The patient is taught to relax and then placed in a trance-like state. Various techniques can then be suggested in order to control symptoms. For example, the patient will be told that his/her abdomen is getting warmer and warmer, and the warmth is helping to ease and soothe the pain like a hot-water bottle. Other techniques can involve getting the patient to visualise the bowel as a large muscular tube that is in spasm. Patients are then told that they can have control over the bowel by relaxing the muscular tube, just as they can relax the muscles in their arms and legs. In addition, the patient is given an audiotape and is expected to practise the technique at home.

The work of Whorwell *et al* (1984) has demonstrated impressive results on selected patients with refractory symptoms, although later work (Whorwell *et al*, 1987) has shown that patients over the age of 50, those with psychiatric symptoms, and those with atypical symptoms respond less favourably. A recent study (Harvey *et al*, 1989), comparing individual hypnosis with group sessions of hypnosis, suggests that group hypnosis may be just as effective as an individual approach, although the numbers in this study were small and there was no reported independent assessment of outcome by a gastroenterologist.

Cognitive–behavioural therapy

The term cognitive–behavioural therapy covers a broad spectrum of treatment approaches (described in Chapter 9). This kind of treatment usually involves relaxation, and techniques to manage stress and anxiety, with specific work to challenge the patient's negative or false beliefs about the nature of his/her symptoms.

This approach has been demonstrated to be effective in new referrals with IBS to a gastrointestinal clinic (Bennett & Wilkinson, 1985). However, there have been no controlled trials involving this kind of psychological approach in patients with refractory symptoms. There is an interesting preliminary report that group stress management in patients with chronic symptoms may be as effective as psychotropic drug treatment (Rumsey *et al*, 1989).

Psychotropic drug treatment

There have been many reports that psychotropic drugs, particularly tricyclic antidepressants, may be effective in patients with IBS. Klein's recent authoritative review, however, suggests that all studies involving psychotropic drug treatment in IBS have been methodologically flawed (Klein, 1988). There are no controlled trials examining the effectiveness of psychotropic drugs in patients with refractory symptoms.

Conclusion

There is mounting evidence that psychological treatment interventions can be effective in patients with refractory IBS. It is not surprising that treatments employing different psychological approaches have similar overall benefits. However, patients with atypical IBS, who complain of constant, unremitting pain, remain, for both the psychiatrist and gastroenterologist, an especially difficult group to manage and treat. It is possible that some such patients might benefit from longer or more intensive psychological treatment approaches than those described above. However, they are often the most reluctant and most difficult patients to engage in psychiatric treatment. Whatever psychological approach is used, it is important to prevent further unnecessary investigation or treatment, particularly surgical intervention. Gastroenterologists and psychiatrists need to collaborate more closely if this is to be achieved.

Acknowledgements

I am grateful to Drs Holmes, Warnes and Braganza, consultant gastroenterologists at Manchester Royal Infirmary, who kindly agreed to allow their patients to participate in this trial. Dr D. Dawson, formerly Senior Registrar in Gastroenterology at Manchester Royal Infirmary, carried out the gastroenterological assessments.

References

BENNETT, P. & WILKINSON, S. (1985) A comparison of psychological and medical treatment of the irritable bowel syndrome. *British Journal of Clinical Psychology*, **24**, 215–216.

GUTHRIE, E. A., CREED, F. H., DAWSON, D., *et al* (1991) A controlled trial of psychological treatment for the irritable bowel syndrome. *Gastroenterology*, **100**, 450–457.

HARVEY, R. F., MAUAUD, E. C. & BROWN, A. M. (1987) Prognosis in the irritable bowel syndrome: a 5-year prospective study. *Lancet*, *i*, 963–965.

——, HINTON, R. A., GUNARY, R. M., *et al* (1989) Individual and group hypnotherapy in treatment of refractory irritable bowel syndrome. *Lancet*, *i*, 424–425.

KINGHAM, J. G. C. & DAWSON, A. M. (1985) Origin of chronic right upper quadrant pain. *Gut*, **26**, 783–788.

KLEIN, K. B (1988) Controlled treatment trials in the irritable bowel syndrome: a critique. *Gastroenterology*, **95**, 232–241.

RUMSEY, N., WILKINSON, S. & WALKER, R. (1989) *A Comparison of Group Stress Management Programmes with Conventional Pharmacological Treatment in the Treatment of the Irritable Bowel Syndrome.* Thurlstone: South Western Gastroenterology Group.

SVEDLUND, J. (1983) Psychotherapy in irritable bowel syndrome: a controlled outcome study. *Acta Psychiatrica Scandinavica*, **67** (suppl. 306), 1–86.

WHORWELL, P. J., PRIOR, A. & FARAGHER, E. B. (1984) Controlled trial of hypnotherapy in the treatment of severe refractory irritable bowel syndrome. *Lancet*, *ii*, 1232–1234.

——, —— & COLGAN, S. C. (1987) Hypnotherapy in severe irritable bowel syndrome: further experience. *Gut*, **28**, 423–425.

9 The cognitive–behavioural approach

PAUL SALKOVSKIS

Patients seek medical advice about physical symptoms for two reasons: (a) inconvenience, disability or pain, (b) anxiety about their cause and outcome. When anxiety is the principal reason for consultation, the patient's problem should be recognised as 'health anxiety' (and, in the most extreme cases, hypochondriasis). However, health anxiety can also occur in association with identifiable physical conditions, and in some cases, may contribute to the origin and maintenance of somatic problems.

This chapter describes recent advances in the understanding and treatment of anxiety disorders in psychiatric practice, using what is known as a cognitive–behavioural approach, and applies them to the management of anxiety about health and anxiety-related physical symptoms.

The cognitive hypothesis proposes that emotions of any kind arise from a person's idiosyncratic interpretation of the meaning of situations and events. For example, someone wakened by a noise in the middle of the night will feel anxious if he/she thinks that there might be an intruder in the house. Similarly, the person who notices palpitations in the middle of the night will become anxious if these are interpreted as signs of an impending heart attack. The quality of the emotional response is determined by the type of interpretation, so the anxiety results from the perception that one is in danger, not from the palpitations *per se*. The particular interpretation depends on factors such as previous experience of and beliefs about illness, and on recent stresses and events, so that identical events produce quite different emotional reactions in different people or even in the same person at different times.

It is the nature of the belief rather than its accuracy that determines the emotional response. Thus, the emotional responses of those who believe they are dying of a heart attack are identical whether this is correct or erroneous. Interpretations not only influence anxiety, but also have important effects on behaviour. In turn, changes in behaviour can modify interpretations. The interplay between interpretations (cognitions) and behaviour has led to this approach being described as 'cognitive–behavioural'.

Excessive and persistent anxiety about health appears to arise from the misinterpretation of three main types of health-related information:

(a) physical sensations and symptoms
(b) bodily variations (of shape, size, and symmetry, including physical signs and normal day-to-day changes in bodily functioning and appearance)
(c) information from other people (including family and medical professionals) and from the mass media.

Misinterpretations and anxiety do not necessarily cause major clinical problems, since they can often be dealt with by brief and accurate reassurance. Difficulties only arise when the misinterpretations and excessive anxiety persist despite medical reassurance. Thus, it is not difficult to understand why some people become anxious about their health; the key question is why this anxiety persists in some individuals despite the best efforts of their doctors. The cognitive hypothesis suggests that a number of feedback mechanisms are involved in persistent anxiety (Fig. 9.1) (Beck *et al*, 1985).

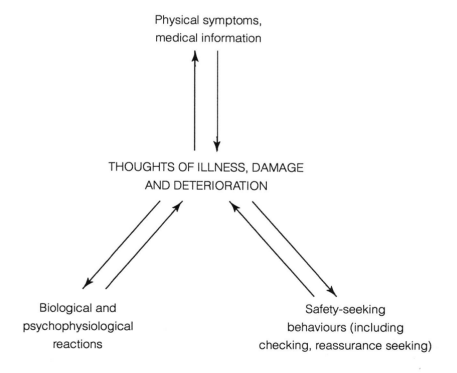

Fig. 9.1. Cognitive model of acute anxiety (after Beck et al, *1985)*

(a) *Triggers of anxiety.* Both physical symptoms and medical information can trigger anxiety; thus a lump under the skin of the neck may be interpreted as a sign of cancer, or an article about the risk of contracting AIDS may lead to the conviction that past behaviour must have led to infection. Once a potential source of threat or danger is identified, the person almost inevitably begins to attend more closely to factors which might be associated with the danger, such as other sites where lumps might occur. This focusing of attention often leads to the 'detection' of other symptoms, apparently confirming the initial fear. Thus, anxious thoughts reinforce the original worries and make them yet more threatening. This phenomenon is well known in medical schools, where 'nosophobia' is common (Ryle, 1947).

(b) *Biological consequences.* Anxiety has biological effects, especially physiological arousal. For example, worry about the possibility of a heart attack can result in an immediate surge in autonomic arousal and to frightening symptoms such as palpitations, tachycardia and breathlessness. This in turn reinforces the original frightening thought. This mechanism is particularly prominent in panic attacks (Salkovskis & Clark, 1986; Clark, 1988; Salkovskis, 1988, 1989, 1990), which commonly accompany hypochondriasis.

(c) *Anxiety-provoked behaviours.* These can increase the severity of symptoms, for example, repeatedly checking an area of inflammation by prodding it in order to see if it is still tender. Again, the consequences of the reaction to anxiety-provoking thoughts are counterproductive, and have the effect of maintaining or even further strengthening the original thoughts.

(d) *Safety-seeking behaviour.* People who strongly believe that they are in danger will usually take steps to ensure their safety. For example, a man who believes that chest pain means that he is about to have a heart attack will stop exercising, and may sit or even lie down. He then sees his survival as evidence (a) that the precautions were wise and effective and (b) that the danger was real and continues. The 'safety-seeking behaviour' therefore prevents the anxious but healthy patient from discovering that his fears are unfounded (Salkovskis, 1991).

In the cognitive hypothesis, these processes are seen as fundamental to the maintenance of threatening illness beliefs and associated anxiety. This concept can be applied to the understanding of the full range of psychological problems seen in a medical setting, some of which are outlined below.

(a) Health anxiety as a normal or exaggerated response to actual physical illness.

(b) Disease phobia, in which patients are disabled by the fear of developing an illness.

(c) Hypochondriasis, the psychiatric condition which typifies anxiety about health. Its essential feature is preoccupation with a belief in or fear of having a serious illness (Warwick & Salkovskis, 1990). This occurs 'without adequate organic pathology' to account for the reaction, and 'despite medical reassurance'. Such fears are associated with the perception of bodily signs and sensations which are mis-interpreted as evidence of serious illness. Primary hypochondriasis is currently a recognised diagnosis in psychiatric diagnostic systems such as DSM–III–R (American Psychiatric Association, 1987).

(d) Less severe and less persistent health anxiety, not fulfilling the criteria for hypochondriasis, which is probably the principal cause of consultation for non-organic physical symptoms.

(e) A number of disorders in which anxiety may play a more or less direct role in the pathophysiology of the disorder (sometimes termed 'psychosomatic' or 'psychophysiological' disorders).

The model shown in Fig. 9.1 can be applied to such disorders. An example is the irritable bowel syndrome (Fig. 9.2). The core health anxiety is that the bowel symptoms are especially threatening, for example, as symptoms of cancer or that ''I may lose control of my bowels''. Any trigger of anxiety, such as news of bowel disease in a relative or a normal twinge of abdominal discomfort, will increase the patient's anxiety about his/her own disorder. This increase in anxiety leads to a physiological response – a further increase of bowel motility – thus exacerbating the symptoms which are most feared. The increased anxiety also leads to behavioural changes, such as changes in use of the lavatory and avoidance of exercise, both of which can increase bowel responsivity. These responses may lead to an increase in the core health anxiety that ''I may lose control of my bowels'', which in turn exacerbates the bowel symptoms. That is to say, the health anxiety is maintained by these responses.

Of course, in many patients, misinterpretation results in only transient anxiety; most do not consistently react in a way which maintains the health anxiety. Examples of factors maintaining persistent anxiety are described in the next section as it is necessary to understand these before psychological treatment can be understood.

Common factors among patients seeking medical help with unexplained physical symptoms

Most patients seeking medical help with unexplained physical symptoms believe that their problems have a physical cause, a belief which may be accurate, exaggerated or completely inaccurate. Although it is not always immediately obvious to the outside observer, patients derive their

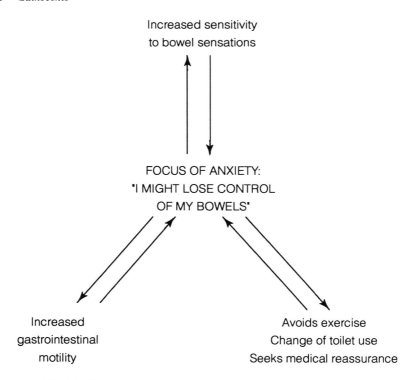

Increased sensitivity
to bowel sensations

FOCUS OF ANXIETY:
"I MIGHT LOSE CONTROL
OF MY BOWELS"

Increased
gastrointestinal
motility

Avoids exercise
Change of toilet use
Seeks medical reassurance

Fig. 9.2. The application of the cognitive model to irritable bowel symptoms

exaggerated or inaccurate beliefs from observations which are internally consistent, and which serve to convince them that their belief is true.

Frequently, the logic of patients' beliefs can be understood in terms of their background, education and experience of illness. Other evidence may arise from the patient's understanding (or misunderstanding) of medical information, for example, the panic patient who is given a diagnosis of 'mitral valve prolapse'. Finally, it must be recalled that problems which originally had a physical cause may later be maintained by psychological factors.

Maintaining factors

Events such as physical symptoms or information from doctors tend to induce anxiety which increases preoccupation with possible illness in at least three ways. These are: increased focus on the body, physiological arousal, and checking behaviour and reassurance-seeking. Subsequent misinterpretation increases the sense of perceived threat, and a vicious circle of anxiety ensues. The following are examples of factors which would maintain such a vicious circle in clinical practice.

(a) *Increased physiological arousal.* A patient noticed an increase in sweating and thought that this was a sign of a serious hormonal imbalance; sweating increased when this thought occurred, which provided further evidence of 'disturbance'. A patient with irritable bowel problems noticed abdominal discomfort and became anxious about losing control of her bowels, which made her stomach churn. Discomfort and pain then increased, resulting in frightening thoughts about incontinence.

(b) *Focus of attention.* A patient noticed that the roots of his fingernails looked pale and that he had white spots on his nails, and interpreted this as a sign of a 'hormone problem'. He found this observation extremely upsetting, and could not believe that he could have previously missed so significant a sign, and that it must therefore be a new phenomenon. This became the focus of his attention; further searching led to increased anxiety. Focus of attention may also lead to changes in physiological systems where both reflex and voluntary control is involved (e.g. breathing, swallowing, muscular activity, etc.). Thus, a patient may notice difficulty in swallowing dry foods and interpret this as a sign of throat cancer. Focusing on swallowing can then lead to repeated swallowing with increased discomfort and difficulty. Similarly, the experience of pain is increased when it becomes the focus of attention (Melzack, 1979) no matter what its cause.

(c) *Avoidant behaviours.* Unlike patients with phobias, patients with worries about their physical condition are primarily anxious about internal bodily symptoms or sensations. Since it is difficult to avoid such anxiety-provoking stimuli patients resort instead to behaviours which aim both to minimise bodily discomfort and to prevent feared disasters. The belief that danger has been averted then sustains the original beliefs. For example ''If I hadn't used my inhaler, I would have suffocated and died'' leads to further use of the inhaler.

Some avoidant behaviours have a more direct physical effect on the patient's symptoms. For example, a patient who noticed persistent weakness reduced his activities, stopped playing sport and reduced the amount he walked. After some months, he noticed that the weakness was getting worse (actually due to unfitness), but saw this as confirming his fears that he was suffering from multiple sclerosis.

(d) *Reassurance seeking.* Bodily checking and reassurance seeking lead to a temporary reduction of anxiety which convinces the patient that this is the best course of action. Unfortunately, this is at the expense of a longer-term increase in anxiety which only leads to further seeking of reassurance. Sometimes, persistent distress and patients' demands persuade sympathetic doctors to offer major medical investigations and treatments. It is the doctor's hope that such investigations will reassure the patient. Unfortunately, patients see such interventions as confirmation of their worst fears of illness, thereby worsening their symptoms and complaints, and sometimes adding new iatrogenic symptoms.

(e) *Misinterpretation of medical information*. Frequently, the most important aspect of health anxiety is the misinterpretation of innocuous bodily changes, and of information provided by doctors, friends or the media. Patients selectively notice and remember information which is consistent with their fears. For instance, a patient saw a neurologist about headaches and dizziness; the neurologist told him that if he had a brain tumour it would have worsened and then killed him. The patient began to notice his symptoms more and concluded that he did indeed have a brain tumour and later told his psychotherapist that the neurologist had said that he had a fatal brain tumour. He believed that the neurologist telling that he had nothing seriously wrong with him was an example of 'breaking it gently'.

Assessment and treatment

The remainder of this chapter describes the psychological treatment of the small but important minority of patients with major and persistent clinical problems, in whom one or more of these maintaining factors may be observed. Psychological treatments have been directed at the three main groups of problems in which there is a significant psychological component.

(a) Observable bodily disturbance, e.g. IBS, hypertension, tics and spasms, asthma, insomnia, sleep-related problems, psychogenic vomiting, eating problems, skin conditions
(b) Primarily perceived symptoms and excessive reactions, e.g. hypochondriasis, somatisation, idiopathic pain, hysterical conversion, dysmorphophobia
(c) Uncertain/mixed physical basis, e.g. headache, temporomandibular joint dysfunction and pain syndrome (TMJDPS), breathlessness, non-organic chest pain (etc.), vestibular problems, tinnitus, chronic pain.

Assessment

A fundamental principle of the cognitive–behavioural approach is that patients' psychological problems should be formulated in positive psychological terms (taking account of any actual physical conditions) rather than by exclusion. A testable and understandable explanation of symptoms agreed with the patient goes a considerable way towards reducing his/her anxiety; the subsequent successful application of the explanation to devise treatment strategies is even more effective. Treatments are then designed to test such working hypotheses and are modified in response to progress or lack of it. The same type of approach can also be applied when the somatic symptoms coexist with other psychological problems (for example depression and loss of appetite; panic attacks and cardiac symptoms (Katon, 1984; Salkovskis, 1989)). In each instance, the psychological formulation is crucial.

The way in which the psychological approach is introduced is important, since many patients believe that they have been wrongly referred for psychological treatment. They believe their problems are entirely physical (and therefore require physical treatment) (Rosenstock & Kirscht, 1979). Such beliefs can make the initial interview particularly difficult, especially if the patient has only agreed to attend in order to convince the therapist that treatment should be medical rather than psychological. One of the therapist's initial tasks must be to discover the patient's attitude to the referral, concentrating particularly on any thoughts the patient may have about its implications. More specific aspects of assessment are discussed elsewhere (Salkovskis, 1989; Warwick & Salkovskis, 1989).

Treatment

The methods described in this chapter are suitable for patients with severe and persistent hypochondriasis; in less severe cases encountered in general practice and hospital settings, less intensive therapy is often effective and elements of this approach might be adopted by GPs. Although the detailed methods of treatment of patients' problems are diverse, the principles shown below apply to most patients, and can be used to facilitate specific treatment techniques.

(a) Aim is to help the patient identify what the problem is, not what the problem is not.

(b) Acknowledge that the symptoms really exist, and that the treatment aims to provide a satisfactory explanation for the symptoms.

(c) Distinguish between giving relevant information and reassuring with irrelevant or repetitive information.

(d) Treatment sessions should never become combative; questioning and collaboration with the patient is the preferred style, as in cognitive therapy in general.

(e) Patients' beliefs are invariably based on evidence which they find convincing; rather than discounting a belief, discover the observations which the patient believes to be evidence of illness and then work collaboratively with the patient on that basis.

(f) Set a limited period contract which fulfils the therapist's requirements while respecting the patient's worries.

(g) The selective attention and suggestibility typical of many patients should be used to demonstrate the way in which anxiety can arise from innocuous circumstances, symptoms and information.

(h) What the patients have understood about what has been said during the treatment sessions must always be checked by asking them to summarise what has been said and its implications for them.

Engagement in treatment

Following a preliminary formulation of the problem, the therapist summarises what the patient has said, emphasising the role of the patient's symptoms, thoughts, beliefs and behaviours, and discusses this account with the patient. The therapist and patient must then agree on treatment goals before treatment can proceed.

Many patients are willing to attend for a psychological assessment, but have a different set of goals from the therapist. Unless these different expectations can be reconciled, therapy is unlikely to be effective. The therapist should not expect patients to 'admit' that their problems are 'just anxiety'. Any impasse can usually be resolved by a discussion which neither rejects the patient's beliefs nor adds weight to them. The therapist must show full acceptance that the patient experiences physical symptoms and that the patient believes they are due to a serious physical illness.

The therapist explains that people generally base such beliefs on particular evidence for which there may be alternative explanations, which will be systematically examined. The patient is explicitly told that this new method of treatment does not include further physical tests and checks, and that reassurance and lengthy discussions of symptoms are not useful.

Before the patient decides whether this new approach to the problem is acceptable, the usefulness of the two alternative ways (new and old) of tackling the problem should be discussed. How long has the patient been trying to solve the problem by exclusively medical means? How effective has this been? Have they ever properly tested the alternative psychological approach now being suggested? It is then suggested that the patient might make a commitment to follow this new psychological approach for four months. If the problem has not improved by a specified date, then it would be reasonable to reconsider the original ways of tackling the problem. In this way, the patients are not asked to give up their view of their problems, but to consider and test an alternative for a limited period. Patients who believe that they may have a physical illness and that it is being neglected usually find this approach to psychological treatment acceptable.

Beginning active treatment

Once the patient has been engaged in treatment, therapy is directed at gathering and testing evidence for a more accurate interpretation of the patients' evidence for physical illness. For example, the patient may say that stopping to sit down relieves chest pain. This observation is then taken up by the patient as evidence that exercise causes the pain, and that rest relieves it. The patient can then be encouraged to review his daily life and may find instances when he exerts himself without pain, and others when pain occurs at rest. This joint exploration of the evidence may lead to a fuller understanding of why the chest pain is not the result of heart disease in a way that bland reassurance cannot. Rather than discounting a belief, the evidence should be discovered and considered with the patient.

At no point should treatment become combative; questioning is the preferred style. If treatment does become confrontational, then the therapist should be seen to be taking the patient's views seriously. For example, if the patient is arguing that chest pains cannot be the result of anxiety, the therapist should not say ''But anxiety often causes chest pains, and yours sounds like that'' but rather ''Right. When you are having chest pains, that you believe cannot be caused by anxiety, do you have any thoughts about what they might be caused by? Is there anything about the chest pains which particularly makes you think they are caused by a heart condition? What is it about the chest pains which makes you think they can't be anxiety?''.

A characteristic feature of hypochondriacal patients is that they selectively attend to information which is consistent with their symptoms and ignore alternative explanations. This other affects the way in which patients understand conversations with others, particularly doctors and other health professionals. It is therefore imperative to check that the patient has accurately understood what the therapist has been saying. This is best done at the end of the session by asking the patient to summarise the important points that have been learned. Finally, the patient should be asked whether he has any worries about what has been discussed during the session. This prevents the therapist inadvertently increasing anxiety and enables any problem to be used as an illustration of the ways in which the patient tends to misinterpret information.

Treatment strategies and reattribution

The principal treatment strategy involves the construction and testing of alternative explanations for the symptoms which are being misinterpreted as signs of physical illness (see Chapter 7). This is done through the use of 'behavioural experiments'. The illness belief is stated as clearly as possible (e.g. ''so your belief is 'I am suffering from multiple sclerosis' '') and the patient is asked to rate on a 0–100 scale (''where 0 is don't believe this at all and 100 is being absolutely convinced it is true''). All the patient's supporting evidence is noted. Alternative explanations are then generated through careful questioning and discussion. The evidence for all alternatives is summarised (often on paper) making sure that therapist and patient agree on the summary. Frequently the first draft of the summary helps generate yet further information. The patient is then asked to re-rate their illness belief on the basis of the alternative explanation. Finally, therapist and patient agree further behavioural assignments, designed to provide further evidence discriminating between the alternative hypotheses, which can be carried out as homework.

Alternative hypotheses

A variety of alternative explanations can be used to account for the symptoms experienced by hypochondriacal patients, based on the maintaining factors mentioned above: physiological arousal, focus of attention, and changes in behaviour. Education is helpful, especially if combined with direct demonstration. This is best done as a provocation of symptoms, e.g. by hyperventilation.

Changing beliefs about the consequences of the problem

Beliefs are modified by several procedures, particularly by discussion of the origin of illness beliefs, self-monitoring (getting the patient to record the occurrence of symptoms, psychological state and significant events), and behavioural experiments (where symptoms are directly manipulated as a demonstration of the way they can be increased or decreased by particular strategies).

Behavioural experiments are a powerful way of changing patients' beliefs about the origin and nature of symptoms. The aim of a behavioural experiment is to demonstrate to patients that their symptoms can be influenced by factors other than those they believe are responsible. For example, a patient who believed that difficulty swallowing was a sign of throat cancer was asked to swallow repeatedly and then describe the effects of this. She was surprised to discover that she found it increasingly difficult to swallow, and that the therapist experienced the same thing when he swallowed repeatedly. Repeated ratings on a 0–100 scale, of the belief ''I have throat cancer'' may change considerably during such an experiment. Interventions of this nature, when the symptom can be reproduced experimentally, have the most impact on behaviour.

Changing behaviour

The majority of behaviour involved in somatic problems is perceived by the patient as serving a preventative or 'safety seeking' function, and is therefore relatively difficult to modify without attention to the underlying beliefs (Salkovskis, 1991). Perhaps the most common of these is seeking reassurance, which constitutes a particular problem in patients anxious about their health.

The counterproductive effects of persistently seeking reassurance can be explained to anxious patients as being similar to 'picking a scab'; it produces short-term relief, but has a longer-term worsening effect. Reassurance includes requests for physical tests, physical examination, or detailed discussion of symptoms in an attempt to rule out possible disease. Most non-anxious patients are relieved by reassurance, but patients who worry about their health respond in a different manner, so that repeated and 'stronger' reassurance becomes counterproductive as the patients selectively attend to and misinterpret the reassurance itself. For example a patient was told, "These headaches are certainly caused by tension; if they persist, then I'll send you for a skull X-ray to put your mind at rest"; he interpreted this as a sign that the doctor believed that he might have a brain tumour.

Repeated attempts to 'prove' to hypochondriacal patients that they are not ill, through either medical tests or verbal persuasion, are most likely to increase anxiety. The ways in which patients seek reassurance vary greatly, including subtle ways, such as 'casual' conversations in which symptoms are mentioned. Several doctors may be consulted simultaneously and friends and families questioned repeatedly, in ways which do not seem to be connected to health worries. As noted earlier, bodily checking is often a prominent feature, and can itself produce problems (e.g. inflammation, pain, tenderness).

The role of seeking reassurance in maintaining problems must be explained in a way that patients can clearly understand. For example, the patient who persistently seeks reassurance and physical investigations could be asked "How long would I have to reassure you today for it to last for the next three months?". Patients usually reply that that is not how reassurance works; it usually works for only a short period. This enables a discussion of the ineffectiveness of reassurance, and the suggestion that longer-lasting alternatives might be worth considering.

When reassurance-seeking is a major and persistent feature of a patient's difficulties, it can be helpful to devise a behavioural experiment demonstrating to the patient the negative effects of reassurance (Salkovskis & Warwick, 1986). This experiment can also function as an engagement strategy in patients who are reluctant to start treatment without a 'final test'. For example, a last physical investigation could be arranged on the strict understanding that it is regarded as unnecessary for the patient's physical health, but may be helpful in the psychological assessment. Self-monitoring of anxiety about health, belief in specific illness-related thoughts, and need for reassurance are all regularly rated on a 0–100 scale before and after the test. If anxiety is reduced in an enduring way, then this is itself helpful. If, as is much more common, anxiety is reduced only briefly, this finding is used as the basis for discussion about the ways in which reassurance exacerbates anxiety. The demonstration also engages the patient in treatment and establishes a collaborative relationship. It provides a clear rationale for controlling the seeking of reassurance and thereby helps the patient to tolerate the initial anxiety caused by behaviour change. Another strategy is to ask patients to specify exactly what procedures would fully convince them that they are not suffering from the feared illness. The therapist then adopts the role of the interested sceptic, asking things like, "Yes, but would that really be convincing? How could you be really sure that the doctor was properly aware of how to use the test?" and so on. This is to illustrate that it is never possible to be certain that illness is not present, in the same way that it is never possible to be sure that a satellite will not fall on our heads as we walk down the street.

Families and others involved with the patient (sometimes including the patient's GP) must be included in treatment and shown how to deal with requests for reassurance. Role-play may be used, in which the patient asks the relative for reassurance and the relative answers (without non-verbal criticism) in previously agreed terms. For example, a relative might reply, ''As we agreed at the clinic, it does not help you if I give you reassurance. I'm not going to respond at all after this''. The relative then either leaves or talks about unrelated things. This type of strategy is usually of little use without the patient's agreement.

Behaviour directly related to the problem

When inappropriate illness behaviour is prominent, treatment aims to demonstrate its role in maintaining anxiety, preoccupation and physiological disturbance. The use of questioning can be helpful, but direct demonstration of the negative effects of behaviour is particularly convincing. The patient and therapist design experiments (a) to test the patient's belief that the behaviour is 'keeping them safe' from serious harm and (b) to see if behaviour which the patient believes relieves symptoms really does so.

For example, a patient was frightened that she had AIDS because she had a number of symptoms which had been reported in the media as characteristic of AIDS. Questioning revealed that she had been particularly frightened by lumps and pain in her neck and axillae. As a result, she frequently prodded and manipulated these areas, resulting in worsening of the pain, with some superficial inflammation and swelling. Patient and therapist then carried out an experiment in which both prodded their necks in the same way for three periods of five minutes during a session. The resulting discomfort and inflammation was sufficient to convince her that her behaviour was responsible for inducing the symptom. Treatment based on methods used in obsessional patients, particularly exposure and response prevention (Salkovskis & Kirk, 1989), appears to be successful in hypochondriacal patients when combined with a cognitive treatment (Salkovskis & Warwick, 1986; Warwick & Salkovskis, 1989, 1990).

Some common problems in treatment

The areas where problems are most likely to emerge are the attitude of the patient towards the likely effects and effectiveness of treatment, and the attitude of other professionals.

Inappropriate expectations of treatment

It is important that the therapist helps the patient to define clear and appropriate treatment goals; these seldom involve a 'cure', and often acknowledge that changes will be slow. Making the targets (and their limitations) explicit early in therapy is helpful, as are regular reviews of progress in which the aims are restated and reformulated. Patients who have over-optimistic expectations of psychological treatment need to adopt a more realistic view. In contrast, when patients are completely hopeless about the prospects of any change, it can be useful to review the ways in which small changes would be helpful in their day-to-day life and then to discuss whether anything would be lost if the patient carried out a small 'experiment' to see if it might be possible to move towards this limited goal. Sometimes it is helpful to make the initial targets overtly psychological (e.g. ''Not to get depressed when I notice I feel dizzy'').

Attitudes of other professionals

The attitudes of other professionals can undermine treatment and careful co-ordination is therefore essential. When colleagues are over-enthusiastic, the patient's expectations can be readily modified. Difficulties are greater when the patient is receiving advice which conflicts with psychological treatment; comments such as ''Don't let anyone tell you that your problem is psychological – it's purely physical''.

Such problems are tackled both by examining the remarks in context, and by liaison with all those involved. It is not helpful to counter-attack by criticising the others' treatment or judgement; patients are usually unable to discriminate between conflicting opinions, and hence have their confidence eroded in both, rightly thinking that such squabbling implies a degree of incompetence. Disagreements between professionals and inconsistent management can increase patients' doubts about the validity of the diagnoses or formulations offered, and hence adversely affect compliance.

Conclusions

The specialist psychological management of severe somatic problems is a challenging undertaking because many patients have chronic, apparently intractable, conditions, and because they are often unwilling to engage in psychologically based treatment. Nevertheless, considerable improvement or total relief is often possible, and even small improvements can make a worthwhile difference to the quality of life. The best results can be expected in patients in whom a major component of their problem relates to anxiety arising from misinterpretation of sensations, signs or external information (e.g. from medical consultations) as evidence of severe illness.

When problems are prolonged and severe, the aims of therapy may have to be limited. Reasonable targets might be (a) gradual improvement over longer periods; (b) bringing about small changes which are helpful to the patient; (c) arresting deterioration; (d) helping the patient lead a fuller life within the constraints of their problem; and (e) reducing distress associated with the problem (anxiety, depression and demoralisation).

Finally, it should be noted that this chapter has concentrated on cognitive–behavioural aspects of treatment. Chronic non-organic problems invariably occur in a complex psychosocial context, and other personal, family and social issues often require specific attention.

Acknowledgements

The author is grateful to the Medical Research Council of the United Kingdom for their support, and to Hilary Warwick and David M. Clark, who have collaborated in the development of this work.

References

AMERICAN PSYCHIATRIC ASSOCIATION (1987) *Diagnostic and Statistical Manual of Mental Disorders* (3rd edn, revised) (DSM–III–R). Washington, DC: APA.

BECK, A. T., EMERY, G. & GREENBERG, R. (1985) *Anxiety Disorders and Phobias: a Cognitive Perspective.* New York: Basic Books.

CLARK, D. M. (1988) A cognitive model of panic attacks. In *Panic: Psychological Perspectives* (eds S. J. Rachman & J. Maser), pp. 71–90. Hillsdale, New Jersey: Lawrence Erlbaum.

KATON, W. (1984) Panic disorder and somatization. *American Journal of Medicine*, **77**, 101–106.

MELZACK, R. (1979) Current concepts of pain. In *Research in Psychology and Medicine* (eds D. J. Oborne, M. M. Gruneberg & J. R. Eiser). London: Academic Press.

ROSENSTOCK, I. M. & KIRSCHT, J. P. (1979) Why people seek health care . In *Health Psychology* (eds G. C. Stone & N. Adler). San Francisco: Jossey Bass.

RYLE, J. A. (1947) Nosophobia. *Journal of Mental Science*, **94**, 1–17.

SALKOVSKIS, P. M. (1988) Phenomenology, assessment and the cognitive model of panic attacks. In *Panic: Psychological Perspectives* (eds S. J. Rachman & J. Maser), pp. 111–136. Hillsdale, New Jersey: Lawrence Erlbaum.

—— (1989) Somatic disorders. In *Cognitive–Behavioural Approaches to Adult Psychological Disorder: A Practical Guide* (eds K. Hawton, P. M. Salkovskis, J. W. Kirk, *et al*), pp. 235–274. Oxford: Oxford University Press.

—— (1990) Panic attacks: cognitive–behavioural treatment. *Psychiatry in Practice*, **9**, 17–21.

—— (1991) The importance of behaviour in the maintenance of panic and anxiety: a cognitive account. *Behavioural Psychotherapy*, **19**, 6–19.

—— & CLARK, D. M. (1986) Cognitive and physiological processes in the maintenance and treatment of panic attacks. In *Panic and Phobias* (eds I. Hand & H. U. Wittchen), pp. 90–103. Heidelberg: Springer Verlag.

—— & WARWICK, H. M. C. (1986) Morbid preoccupations, health anxiety and reassurance: a cognitive behavioural approach to hypochondriasis. *Behaviour Research and Therapy*, **24**, 597–602.

—— & KIRK, J. (1989) Obsessional problems. In *Cognitive–Behavioural Approaches to Adult Psychological Disorder: A Practical Guide* (eds K. Hawton, P. M. Salkovskis, J. W. Kirk, *et al*), pp. 129–168. Oxford: Oxford University Press.

WARWICK, H. M. C. & SALKOVSKIS, P. M. (1989) Cognitive therapy of hypochondriasis. In *Cognitive Therapy in Clinical Practice* (eds J. Scott, J. M. C. Williams & A. T. Beck), pp. 78–102. London: Croom Helm.

—— & —— (1990) Hypochondriasis. *Behaviour Research and Therapy*, **28**, 105–118.

10 Antidepressants and their role in chronic pain: an update

CHARLOTTE FEINMANN

Soon after the monoamine oxidase inhibitors (MAOIs) were introduced as antidepressant therapy, Webb & Lascelles (1961) noted that tranylcypromine relieved the facial pain associated with some cases of chronic depression. In order to avoid the dietary restrictions and potentially severe interactions of MAOIS, a tricyclic antidepressant drug, amitriptyline, has been used for a wide range of psychogenic and idiopathic facial pains. These pains include facial arthromyalgia (temporomandibular joint dysfunction syndrome), atypical facial pain, that is to say, a chronic idiopathic non-muscular pain which does not involve the joints, atypical odontalgia and the oral dysaesthesias including glossodynia. Amitriptyline, despite its sedative effects, proved to be successful in relieving pain.

Later, in a double-blind controlled trial of the tricyclic antidepressant, dothiepin, 71% of patients were relieved of their pain after nine weeks compared with 46% on placebo (Feinmann & Harris, 1984). Furthermore, this action appeared to be independent of any antidepressant effect. Only 33% of the pain patients were depressed, and this was probably secondary to their pain in many cases. The majority (55%) of cases were psychiatrically normal. This ability of tricyclics to relieve chronic pain in psychiatrically normal non-depressed individuals has been confirmed by Sharav et al (1987).

Tricyclic antidepressants are now also used in the management of tension headache (Diamond & Baltes, 1971), chronic recurrent migraine (Couch & Hassanein, 1979), back and pelvic pain, and pruritus (Alcoff et al, 1982), all of which occur in association with facial arthromyalgia and atypical facial pain. Additional non-psychiatric uses include nocturnal enuresis, where the action is probably a combination of sedation, anticholinergic effect and the regulation of sleep. These drugs are also used for the pain of neurogenic diabetic neuropathy (Sindrup et al, 1990), post-herpetic neuralgia (Leijou & Boivie, 1989), and as an adjunct to the management of terminal pain (Broadfield, 1984) as well as the enigmatic conditions myalgic encephalo-myelitis, and primary fibromyalgia (Caruso et al, 1987).

TABLE 10.1
Side-effects of selected antidepressants

	Sedative	Anticholinergic
Nortriptyline	low	low
Desimipramine	low	low
Doxepin	high	medium
Dothiepin	medium	medium
Imipramine	medium	medium
Protriptyline	low	high
Trimipramine	high	medium
Amitriptyline	high	high

Confusion, prejudice and ignorance surround the use of antidepressants to treat chronic facial pain. The analgesic effect is sometimes attributed, without any supporting evidence, to the relief of depressed mood, apparent or masked. Other theories such as the correction of disturbed sleep pattern, or the relaxation of tensed muscles, remain possible but unproven. Disastrous side-effects are reported by those practitioners unfamiliar with the routine prescription of antidepressant medication (Table 10.1). An additional problem is the confusion between the non-addictive tricyclics and the highly addictive benzodiazepines.

Aetiology of the pain

Idiopathic facial pain may arise

(a) as a manifestation of stress in an otherwise fit person
(b) as a symptom of psychiatric illness such as anxiety or depression
(c) as a feature of an inbuilt personality trait (Sternbach, 1976; Feinmann & Harris, 1984).

Unfortunately, the clinical presentation is similar whatever the aetiology. It may be a transient disturbance without psychiatric disorder or part of a range of abnormal illness behaviours. In either case, the symptoms may vary from a dull ache affecting only the temporomandibular joint and its musculature, to marked pain and discomfort throughout the facial bones, teeth, tongue and oral mucosa.

As already stated, facial pain is not the only symptom. Recurrent symptoms such as tension headache, migraine and neckache, low back pain, pelvic pain, menorrhagia, irritable bowel syndrome and pruritic skin disturbance are also reported by 80% of patients. The prevalence of these symptoms suggests a constitutional vulnerability to develop such complaints. Furthermore, although only 33% of patients are found to be depressed, 80% report a stressful life event within six months of the onset of pain.

Stressful life events may create pain directly or make it more likely that the subject seeks help for previous discomfort.

Psychiatric symptoms appear to develop in those made vulnerable by a deprived childhood, a neurotic personality and poor social adjustment. When present, psychiatric symptoms are often mild, of brief duration and are best considered to be part of a normal reaction to distress. The close association between chronic pain, adverse life events and long-term problems emphasise the need for a thorough clinical assessment of a patient's problem, and for conservative forms of management. It is vital to emphasise to the patient that the pain is real, not imaginary, but arising in cramped muscles and blood vessels as a response to stress. Patients who do not respond to reassurance should then be treated with antidepressants in slowly increasing doses.

Mode of action

It has been suggested that pharmacological similarities exist between tricyclic antidepressants and centrally acting analgesics. Stress-induced excessive or irrelevant muscular activity or vascular dysfunction are useful models of a peripheral endorgan dysfunction. But the most popular explanation for the action of antidepressants on pain is the effect on synaptic levels of serotonin and noradrenaline. Sternbach (1976) has postulated that, once established, chronic pain depletes the level of neurotransmitters, particularly serotonin, in the area of the dorsal raphe nucleus. This area is considered crucial in pain suppressor pathways. This depletion may account for the apparent ineffectiveness of analgesics in chronic pain, and the association of chronic pain with depression. Hence the ability of tricyclic antidepressants to improve both. The newer antidepressants such as mianserin and viloxazine appear at present to have either equivocal or no demonstrable analgesic activity and zimeldine, a 5-HT reuptake inhibitor, is only reported by Johansson & Knorring (1979) to have an effect superior to placebo.

Despite the suggested mode of action, drugs with a predominant serotonin antagonist action, such as zimeldine, appear to have the worst reputation for side-effects. Although von Knorring *et al* (1978) suggested that patients with somatoform pain disorders benefit from treatment with antidepressants with a strong effect on serotonin rather than noradrenaline reuptake, there is little evidence to support this. Tricyclics with an intact tertiary amine group (e.g. amitriptyline, clomipramine) are said to show better analgesic activity than demethylated substances such as nortriptyline and desimipramine (Budd, 1978). France (1987) stated that no one drug has been shown to be superior in relieving pain; drug selection is based on matching the side-effect profile of each agent with each individual patient's needs. Results of controlled studies do not seem to show any difference between the efficacy of the more serotonergic antidepressants and the more noradrenergic (Stimmel & Escobar, 1986). The intimate interaction between serotonergic and noradrenergic mechanisms has been demonstrated (Proudfit, 1977) and it is possible that both serotonin and noradrenaline are involved in the analgesic activity of antidepressants (Hwang & Wilcox, 1987).

Tricyclic antidepressants have been shown to potentiate the effects of narcotic analgesics such as morphine, lending support to the suggestion that they potentiate naturally occurring endorphins in blood and/or cerebrospinal fluid (Biegon & Samuel, 1980). In addition, subnormal endorphin function has been reported in patients with chronic pain (von Knorring *et al*, 1978; Facchieretti *et al*, 1981). Recent evidence from patients with post-operative pain (Levine *et al*, 1986) and from animal models of chronic pain (Testa *et al*, 1987) has confirmed that the analgesic activity of antidepressants is partly related to their modulating effect on endogenously released opioid peptides.

Studies of the anti-nociceptive effect of antidepressants in animals have yielded conflicting results, both in the tail flick test and in the hot plate test. The tail flick test, which is one of the most commonly used nociceptive tests, has been shown to be sensitive to changes in tail skin temperature. A negative correlation is consistently found between tail flick latency and tail skin temperature. Tricyclic antidepressants may change blood flow and thereby skin temperature of the tail, and may furthermore influence tail skin temperature by reducing stress hyperthermia or by reducing locomotor activity (Lund *et al*, 1989).

The action of tricyclic antidepressants on pain appears to be independent of any antidepressant effect, and analgesia may occur at doses lower than those which would be used for depression (Hameroff *et al*, 1982). Furthermore, tricyclics are reported to relieve the pain in a much shorter time than that needed for relief of depressive symptoms (Goodman & Charney, 1985). The interaction of drug therapy and psychotherapy is complex. For example, Pilowsky & Barrow (1990) have recently shown that reported intensity of pain increases as a result of psychotherapy.

Treatment regime

In our clinical practice, tricyclic antidepressants are not used in isolation. A pragmatic treatment approach is adopted in which the diagnosis is first established by a careful history which identifies other psychosomatic pains and seeks out stressful life events. The patient is then reassured that no serious illness is present, counselled in terms of lifestyle, and medication is prescribed in slowly increasing doses.

Tricyclic antidepressants should be taken at night in slowly increasing doses, combined with regular review at three- to six-weekly intervals to provide reassurance and achieve compliance. As sedation is not required in most cases, a drug with low sedative and low anticholinergic side-effects, such as nortriptyline, is recommended. Nortriptyline may be increased gradually from 10 to 30 mg then from 50 to 100 mg.

For patients with insomnia, a sedating drug such as dothiepin is useful, starting at a single night-time dose of 25 mg, and increasing in steps up to 225 mg at night when necessary. In elderly patients with constipation and glaucoma, and in males with prostatic hypertrophy, the least anticholinergic drug should be prescribed. Combinations of drugs such as nortriptyline and a phenothiazine are useful when the patient's pain is accompanied by extreme anxiety or bizarre symptoms. Trifluoperazine 2 mg three times a day (t.d.s.) or flupenthixol or fluphenazine 0.5 mg t.d.s. may be used and increased as the symptoms dictate.

Stoicism is required on the part of the clinician, as those patients for whom medication is most essential are more resistant to this management and complain of more side-effects than others. The side-effects are often bizarre and incapacitating. In one of our studies there were more side-effects in the placebo group than with the active drug! Pain recurrence is sometimes associated with withdrawal of medication and in some cases medication has to be continued for up to a year to prevent relapse. Once the patient has confidence in the clinician and the medication, and has been free from pain for two or three months, the medication can usually be reduced without problems.

The principal difficulty is convincing these patients that they require support and medication as opposed to surgery. The willingness of patients to accept operative intervention, which may contribute to rendering their condition intractable, emerges in refractory cases. The management of intractable facial pain remains a challenge, especially where the condition appears to have been reinforced by previous, irrelevant surgery (Feinmann & Harris, 1984). These patients are best admitted to hospital for a supervised regime of a phenothiazine such as flupenthixol or trifluoperazine, together with the tricyclic drug. Occasionally a combination of the tricyclic drug with a monoamine oxidase inhibitor is valuable for severe intractable pain, despite misconceptions about their interactions.

Conclusion

The medical management of chronic pain may often be highly effective and clinically valuable. The introduction of novel formulations specifically designed for pain management will increase the use of antidepressants to treat chronic pain as they overcome the problems that some clinicians have experienced with tricyclic antidepressants.

References

ALCOFF, J., JONES, E., REST, P., *et al* (1982) A controlled trial of imipramine for low back pain. *Journal of Family Practice*, 14, 841–846.

BIEGON, A. & SAMUEL, P. (1980) Interaction of tricyclic antidepressants with opiate receptors. *Biochemical Pharmacology*, 29, 460–462.

BROADFIELD, M. (1984) The treatment of cancer pain. *Continuing Practise*, 11, 17–26.

BUDD, K. (1978) Psychotropic drugs in the treatment of chronic pain. *Anesthesia*, 33, 531–534.

CARUSO, I., PUTTINI, P. C., BOCCASSIN, P., *et al* (1987) Double blind study of dothiepin versus placebo in the treatment of primary fibromyalgia syndrome. *Journal of International Medical Research*, 15, 154–159.

COUCH, J. R. & HASSANEIN, R. S. (1979) Amitriptyline in migraine prophylaxis. *Archives of Neurology*, 36, 695–699.

DIAMOND, S. & BALTES, B. J. (1971) Chronic tension headache treated with amitriptyline, a double blind study. *Headache*, 11, 110–116.

FACCHIERETTI, I., NAPP, G., SAROLTI, F., *et al* (1981) Primary headaches: reduced circulating β liposophin β endorphin levels with impaired reactivity to acupuncture. *Cephalgia*, 1, 195–201.

FEINMANN, C. & HARRIS, M. (1984) Psychogenic facial pain: part II management and prognosis. *British Dental Journal*, 156, 165–168.

FRANCE, R. D. (1987) The future for antidepressants: treatment of pain. *Psychopathology*, 20 (suppl. 1), 99–113.

GOODMAN, W. K. & CHARNEY, D. S. (1985) Therapeutic applications and mechanisms of action by monoamine oxidase inhibitors and heterocyclic antidepressant drug. *Journal of Clinical Psychiatry*, 46, 6–26.

HAMEROFF, S., CORK, R., SHERER, K., *et al* (1982) Doxepin effects on chronic pain, depression and plasma opioids. *Journal of Clinical Psychiatry*, 42, 22–26.

HWANG, A. & WILCOX, G. L. (1987) Analgesic properties of intrathecally administered heterocyclic antidepressants. *Pain*, 28, 343–355.

JOHANNSSON, F. & KNORRING, L. V. (1979) A double-blind study of a serotonergic uptake inhibitor (zimeldine) versus placebo in chronic pain patients. *Pain*, 7, 69–78.

LEIJOU, G. & BOIVIE, J. (1989) Central post stroke pain – a controlled trial of amitriptyline and carbamazepine. *Pain*, 36, 126–136.

LEVINE, J. P., CARDON, N. C. & SMITH, R. (1986) Desimipramine. Enhances opiate post-operative analgesia. *Pain*, 27, 45–49.

LUND, A., TJOLSEN, A. & KJELL, H. (1989) The apparent antinociceptive effect of desimipramine and imipramine in the tail flick test in rats is mainly caused by change in tail skin temperature. *Pain*, 38, 65–69.

PILOWSKY, I. & BARROW, G. C. (1990) A controlled study of psychotherapy and amitriptyline used individually and in combination in the treatment of chronic intractable psychogenic pain. *Pain*, 40, 3–19.

PROUDFIT, H. K. (1977) Pharmacological evidence for the modulation of nociception by noradrenergic neurones. In *Pain Modulation Progress in Brain Research* (eds H. L. Field & J. M. Besson), pp. 357–370. Amsterdam: Elsevier.

SHARAV, Y., SINGER, E., SCHMIDT, E., *et al* (1987) The analgesic effect of amitriptyline on chronic pain. *Pain*, 31, 199–209.

SINDRUP, H. S., *et al* (1990) The selective serotonin reuptake inhibitor paroxetine is effective in the treatment of diabetic neuropathy symptoms. *Pain*, 42, 135–144.

STERNBACH, R. (1976) The need for an animal model of chronic pain. *Pain*, 2, 2–4.

STIMMEL, G. L. & ESCOBAR, J. J. (1986) Antidepressants in chronic pain: a review of efficacy. *Pharmacology*, 6, 262–267.

TESTA, R., ANGELICA, P. & ABBATI, G. A. (1987) Effect of citalopran, amineptine, imipramine and nortriptyline on stress-induced analgesia in rats. *Pain*, 29, 247–255.

VON KNORRING, L., ALMAY, B. G. L., JOHANNSON, I., *et al* (1978) Pain perception and endorphin levels in cerebrospinal fluid. *Pain*, 5, 359–385.

WEBB, H. E. & LASCELLES, R. G. (1961) Treatment of official head pain associated with depression. *Lancet*, i, 355–356.

Appendix: Conference discussion

The general discussion at the end of the day was surprisingly uncontroversial. Fellows and members from both Colleges agreed that the clinical problem presented by patients with symptoms not due to organic disease was large and important, and that the provision of better care would require changes in medical behaviour and in the training of both physicians and psychiatrists, as well as a closer collaboration with general practitioners (GPs). There was also agreement about the need for an approach to treatment which recognised the genuine nature of the patients' symptoms, and in which appropriate medical investigation and psychological assessment were pursued in parallel. Criticism of each other's specialty was less conspicuous than arguments for joint solutions in the individual clinic and hospital and for collaboration between the two Colleges to promote training, and more research to develop and evaluate effective treatments.

Management in the medical clinic

It was clear that there is great variability in the interest and capabilities of physicians dealing with non-organic physical problems. Several themes were emphasised by a number of speakers:

(a) The need to restrict investigations to those for which there are specific indications. There is still a general assumption that it is worse to miss an inoperable cancer than to miss a treatable psychogenic illness.

(b) Physicians must be sympathetic towards these types of problem, and be willing to accept symptoms as genuine and in need of treatment.

(c) Treatment should be directed to helping patients understand the underlying cause of their symptoms and the necessity of making the appropriate changes in their lives to relieve the symptoms and prevent them from recurring. Such treatment does not rely on telling patients what to do but requires understanding of the patient's beliefs, and time for discussion. Psychological therapy is unlikely to be effective if the patient does not feel in control. The patient and the therapist should share knowledge and information. Patients should be at liberty to use or not use the treatment that is offered. This may be very different from the traditional doctor/patient interactions in some medical out-patient clinics.

(d) Precise methods of treatment are likely to vary with the type of physical symptom. It seems that antidepressants are particularly appropriate for a number of pain syndromes, such as facial pain or headache, even if there are no major depressive symptoms. Other symptoms, such as chest pain and palpitations, are commonly associated with generalised anxiety and with panic attacks, and frequently respond to standard psychological treatment for anxiety. Explanation and reassurance appears to be often effective in neurological out-patient clinics, but is less successful in cardiac clinics.

In planning services, it is essential to be clear about what physicians and surgeons are willing to do themselves. Only a very small proportion of the enormous number of patients concerned will be referred to a psychiatrist. Physicians, GPs and their teams have to cope with the vast majority. They need to consider:

(a) what can best be done by the physician with appropriate skills and limited time;
(b) the role of the GP;
(c) which problems need the extra skills and extra time which can only be provided by psychiatrists or by clinical psychologists.

Many physicians felt that they would like to be able to do more themselves and use briefer forms of psychological treatment. There was some interest in the increased use of specialist nurses and other members of the medical team who might have more time than the physician. The availability of pain clinics was seen to be important for the subgroup with chronic pain.

The use of antidepressant medication

A number of questions dealt with the use of antidepressant medication by physicians. Several speakers stressed the value of the routine use of low-dosage antidepressants in the treatment of certain unexplained symptoms, such as facial pain and some other pain syndromes.

There was less confidence about the treatment of patients with depressive symptoms. Psychiatrists emphasised the need to recognise and treat major depressive disorder. Physicians should be more aware that this is a syndrome in which depression itself is often less prominent than a wide range of other symptoms (lack of energy, fatigue, poor sleep, irritability, loss of weight and appetite, lack of pleasure in life, pessimism). A smiling facade and denial of misery often conceal depressive symptoms.

It was agreed that physicians should be able to treat depression with an appropriate antidepressant; they should certainly be confident in prescribing tricyclics and one or two newer antidepressants, but because of their risk, monoamine oxidase inhibitors should be seen as a specialist treatment. It is always important to encourage patients to persevere. Some sort of check on compliance with medication is useful.

Failure to respond to antidepressant medications should initially lead to an increase in dosage. A referral should be made to a psychiatrist when the depression is severe, or when it is resistant to the physician's treatment. The patient should be told: "we do not seem to be satisfactorily treating your symptoms, I think we should have another specialist opinion".

The role of psychiatrists and clinical psychologists

Physicians complained about the frequent lack of immediate or early availability of a psychiatrist, and about psychiatrists who wrote back saying "no psychiatric disorder found". It was agreed that psychiatrists, like physicians, must alter their attitudes to the management of these patients.

Some general hospitals have consultation–liaison psychiatrists whose job should include working out with the physicians the ways in which they can best help. This often involves attending physicians' meetings and giving talks at their research clubs. In this way, physicians and psychiatrists can educate each other as to the sort of patients who will benefit from referral, and how the referral is brought about.

One psychiatrist described how in the early stages of working together, when physician and psychiatrist do not know each other well, it is often the most intractable hypochondriacal patients who are referred. The psychiatrist frequently finds these patients just as difficult to help as did the referring physician. This failure can lead to an early confirmation of the false premise that "psychiatrists cannot help these patients any more than I can". Both parties must survive this difficult initial period, so that a better understanding of which patients can be appropriately referred and helped develops. The referral rate then seems to settle down at an appropriate level; referrals are made of patients whom the physician finds difficult to manage, and to whom the psychiatrist can offer some constructive advice and treatment.

Through such liaison, the physician often acquires more skill in prescribing antidepressant drugs and more confidence in providing psychological explanations for non-organic symptoms when appropriate. A psychiatrist learns how to make treatment acceptable and effective. Sometimes, this increased acknowledgement of psychological factors leads to a decrease in referrals to the psychiatrist. If the referral rate rises or falls significantly, the reasons for this can be discussed between the two parties.

There was considerable interest in the role of the clinical psychologist, either working in the medical clinic, or as an alternative to referral to a psychiatrist. However, few physicians had had experience of working with psychologists. One member of the audience commented on the multidisciplinary approach in many pain clinics and suggested this model could be more widely applied.

Making a referral

If the physician feels unable to cope with the emotional demands of the patient, or if he feels unable to offer effective treatment, then referral to a psychiatrist is appropriate. The size and nature of the group of patients referred to a psychiatric opinion depend on the physician's skills and on whether there is a suitable psychiatrist to whom the patient may be referred. A good working relationship between the physician and a psychiatrist holding clinics in the general hospital makes referral easier. It becomes a routine procedure for a common medical problem rather than an admission of medical failure.

A particularly difficult subgroup of patients are those with multiple hypochondriacal complaints, who may be attending several clinics, and who have long histories of unsuccessful medical treatment and investigation. For these patients, the aim of referral to a psychiatrist may be damage limitation rather than cure. Simplifying medical care so as to avoid the iatrogenic complications of unnecessary referrals is clinically valuable. The liaison psychiatrist needs to discuss with the individual physician the ways in which he/she can refer patients, minimising the effects of the stigma that is often still attached to attendance at a psychiatric clinic. One psychiatrist outlined the explanation he had suggested to a cardiologist colleague seeing patients with non-cardiac chest pain: ''I acknowledge that you have chest pain and other symptoms. They are not due to treatable disease or other major medical illness, but they are real symptoms and we need a definite idea of their cause if we are to treat them satisfactorily. I think you ought to see a colleague of mine who works in this hospital, who has a lot of experience in dealing with these sort of problems and whom I think will be able to help you.''

The role of the general practitioner

A GP noted that he and his colleagues in primary care are actually doing much of what had been discussed. They frequently treat the medical and psychiatric aspects of problems simultaneously, referring only a small proportion of patients with psychiatric disorders to specialists. Since most psychological distress is handled in the GP's surgery, it is often most appropriate for physicians to refer patients with non-organic physical problems straight back to the GP, avoiding the complexity of psychiatric referral.

Other speakers agreed that referral back to the GP was often sensible, but they noted that not all GPs have the skills and time to manage the more complicated and persistent problems. Improved training for GPs would give the general practice team an even greater role.

Complementary medicine

One participant suggested that complementary medicine has a role to play with this group of patients, arguing that one advantage of this approach is that it allows patients to take back more responsibility for themselves and in that way gain control over their destiny, rather than depending on an antidepressant or some similar treatment. He had often noticed that such patients report feeling pleased that they have been able to help themselves. Subsequent speakers were more cautious, outlining the continuing responsibility of the GP in reviewing his/her patient's progress and in dealing with problems as they arose.

Training

Several speakers noted that most medical students are interested in the whole person rather than in organ diseases, but that this interest is often lost at the junior doctor stage because of the heavy workload, tiredness and lack of encouragement. There was considerable discussion of how we should encourage, rather than discourage, junior (and senior) doctors in this aspect of their work.

Physicians

It was felt that physicians do not need specialist psychiatric expertise for most of the vast numbers of patients with non-organic physical symptoms that they see in district hospitals. However, they do need more training. Professor Goldberg had already demonstrated at the conference that training material exists; it was felt that a decision by physicians to adapt and incorporate this into their own training programmes was needed.

Psychiatrists

It is essential that the psychiatrists are more sympathetic towards this type of referral. Senior psychiatrists whose previous experience has been with the seriously mentally ill may need extra training so that they can assess and treat people who come to their clinics claiming there is no psychological problem. To declare that no formal psychiatric disorder is present is totally inadequate. More training is also essential for young psychiatrists, both through formal teaching and through experience of working in the general hospital settings.

Medical students

Speakers believed that a greater emphasis is needed on training medical students to manage non-organic physical symptoms. We need to teach students that a brief psychiatric assessment of patients who present with physical symptoms can be rewarding. The emphasis should be on encouraging medical students and young doctors to acquire the skills to treat these patients themselves. At the same time, they require the example and enthusiasm of senior doctors and of professional organisations, such as the Royal Colleges.

Conclusions

It was acknowledged that most of the material presented at the meeting was not particularly recondite and was well known to one or other half of the audience but, unfortunately, not often known to both parties at the same time. A number of practical suggestions were made.

(a) Audit groups and the district postgraduate tutor should meet to find out what specialist psychiatric service is on offer. If this is inadequate, they should try to fill the gap.

(b) Both Royal Colleges should improve their training and recommendations for services for this group of patients.

(c) Several physicians said there was a desperate need for more psychiatrists with an interest in liaison psychiatry. At present, there is frequently no one to turn to for help with these patients. The President of the Royal College of Psychiatrists responded: ''If you feel the need for a liaison psychiatrist and do not have one, it would be very helpful if you could make your case to the new purchaser, the District Health Authority. If the purchasers recognise that physicians require the assistance of an interested and adequately trained psychiatrist, this will strengthen the case for improving the manpower situation. Only once there are an adequate number of suitably trained psychiatrists can we provide the service that patients need.''

(d) The conference was concerned about how to provide help for large numbers of patients. Only a small proportion can be referred to psychiatrists. The number of potential referrals is limited by the number of psychiatrists with appropriate skills. Similarly, there are few clinical psychologists. One answer might be specially trained nurses working in medical clinics with some supervision by a psychiatrist or a psychologist.

(e) The concern among discussants about the significance of the clinical problem, manpower, and training of both physicians and psychiatrists led to support for a joint working party between the two Colleges to ensure this issue is carried forward.

Psychiatrists pointed out that the expansion of liaison psychiatry may not be easily achieved, as most psychiatrists are preoccupied at present with providing a community service. A recent survey of district psychiatric services indicated that more than 60% planned to develop a community mental health service, but less than 14% had plans to improve their liaison psychiatry services. Planners of psychiatric services need to be convinced of the case for putting more manpower and training resources into this specialised area, in order to provide the service that physicians require.

Index

Compiled by STANLEY THORLEY